Correspondence
1943–1955

THEODOR W. ADORNO
AND THOMAS MANN

Correspondence
1943–1955

Edited by Christoph Gödde
and Thomas Sprecher
Translated by Nicholas Walker

polity

First published in German as *Briefwechsel: 1943–1955* of Theodor W. Adorno and Thomas Mann and © Suhrkamp Verlag, Frankfurt am Main, 2002.

This English translation © Polity Press, 2006.

Polity Press
65 Bridge Street
Cambridge CB2 1UR, UK

Polity Press
350 Main Street
Malden, MA 02148, USA

ISBN-10: 0-7456-3200-9
ISBN-13: 978-07456-3200-9

A catalogue record for this book is available from the British Library.

Typeset in 10.5 on 12pt Sabon
by Servis Filmsetting Ltd, Manchester
Printed and bound in India by
Replika Press Pvt Ltd.

For further information on Polity, visit our website: www.polity.co.uk

The publication of this work was supported by a grant from the Goethe-Institut.

Contents

Editors' Note

Thomas Mann's correspondence with Theodor W. Adorno was preceded and effectively prompted by his reading the philosopher's work. In July 1943, while he was working on chapter 7 of his novel *Doctor Faustus*, Mann was also studying Adorno's manuscript on 'Schönberg and Progress'. 'I encountered an artistic and sociological critique of our current situation of the most subtle, progressive and profound kind, and one which displayed a striking affinity to the central conception of my own work, to the very "composition" in which I was then immersed and involved. The matter was soon decided. "This is my man"' (*Die Entstehung des Doktor Faustus*, *GW* XI, p. 172). The relationship between tradition and avant-garde culture, the constellation of modernity and the past, defines the forcefield of Mann's novel as well as that of Adorno's investigations of the dialectic of technological progress in music. These representatives of two different generations, with significantly different cultural and aesthetic backgrounds in each case, recognized a remarkable closeness to one another that subsequently led, over and beyond their specifically literary and musical collaboration, to a periodically renewed exchange of letters that touched repeatedly on broader social and political issues as well.

Adorno's manuscript on Schoenberg provided the initial stimulus for a rapidly developing social and intellectual relationship between the philosopher and the writer. Personal invitations and mutual visits led to detailed discussions concerning both the composition of the whole novel and very specific musical details, such as those involved in Wendell Kretzschmar's lectures on Beethoven in chapter 8 of the book. On 30 December 1945, when his narrative was approaching the subject of Adrian Leverkühn's late works, Mann wrote his famous letter on 'the principle of montage' in *Doctor Faustus*, explicitly inviting Adorno to 'consider, with me, how such a work – and I mean Leverkühn's work – could more or less be practically realized'. Adorno, having already examined the manuscript of the novel up to this point in the narrative, proceeded to sketch examples of Leverkühn's final compositions, which Mann then 'versified', as he put it, developing and incorporating these ideas into the body of the novel – ideas which, as models of Adorno's 'exact imagination', give the lie to any blank or abstract opposition between the original sketch and the finished novel. In a letter to Erika Mann of 19 April 1962, Adorno described the nature of his collaboration with the writer in the following way:

> Finally, a word concerning Leverkühn's musical compositions. It turned out that T. M. had already chosen the titles for most of the works in question which he immediately communicated to me; I then set about thinking them out in detail. I think it was only with the Brentano songs that we did not proceed in this fashion, and in this case I didn't go beyond giving some general musical suggestions. As for the rest, it was extremely straightforward: I thought about the problems exactly as I would have done as a composer actually confronted with the task of writing such works, just as someone, like Berg for example, would generally prepare a plan before setting to work. I noted down the relevant considerations, and still possess a number of these sketches, before proceeding to elaborate them as if there were not merely preparatory outlines, but descriptions of real pieces of music. T. M. would then contribute his own part. Many things would be changed in the course of our discussions, whether it was a matter of developing the overall conception of the novel more concretely through the description of specific musical details, or of emphasizing alternative aspects and features of the narrative, as in the chapter on the Devil, or whether finally, and this is the most important point, it was a question of cutting a number of things precisely because the work in hand was a novel rather than a musical guide book. I do not believe that his conception of these afternoon discussions, of which I naturally possess the clearest and most precise recollection, would have differed in any way whatsoever from my own.

Even more than Thomas Mann, who was fascinated by the 'striking affinity' between the aesthetic ground-plan of his novel and Adorno's avant-garde aesthetic, Adorno himself must have regarded this effective collaboration as an epitome of his own utopian conception of knowledge – namely the construction of a concrete form of understanding that successfully reconciles the conceptual and the intuitive moments of experience through an activity of productive imagination.

Although relatively few of the letters exchanged between Mann and Adorno belong precisely to the period in which *Doctor Faustus* was actually completed, their active collaboration with regard to the putative compositions of the novel's protagonist Adrian Leverkühn nonetheless formed the basis and point of departure for their subsequent correspondence as well. Mann would later report back to Adorno about his 'fascinated reading' of *Minima Moralia* and respond in detail to the *Essay on Wagner,* a work which he confessed he was as eager to read as 'the one in the Book of Revelation who consumes a book which tastes "as sweet as honey"'. Adorno in turn communicated his own detailed comments upon, and enthusiastic support for, Mann's later novels such as *The Holy Sinner, The Black Swan* and *The Confessions of Felix Krull* – the last work being particularly close to Adorno's heart. The letters also addressed extremely private concerns of great personal significance to both of them, as in the candid and carefully considered discussion of the difficulties involved in returning to Europe after the end of the war. Although they were destined never to meet again in person after the autumn of 1949, when Adorno returned to Germany, their continuing correspondence testifies to their persisting mutual concern for and interest in one another. Adorno always remained faithful to his personal encounter with Mann, something which he himself described in his letter of 3 June 1945 on commemoration of the writer's seventieth birthday as 'a moment of realized utopia'.

The editors of the present volume have benefited from the opportunity of consulting the transcription of, and a provisional and incomplete commentary upon, Thomas Mann's letters prepared by Prof. Dr Hans Wysling and Beatrice Trummer in the early 1990s. The current editors remain responsible for any errors in this edition of the correspondence.

At present the original letters from Adorno to Mann are preserved in the Thomas Mann Archive in Zurich. The original letters from Mann to Adorno are preserved in the Adorno Archive in Frankfurt. In a number of cases, where Adorno's letters have not survived in the Mann Archive, the transcription has been based upon the carbon copies of the originals in the Adorno Archive. The same procedure has been employed for the transcription of the texts printed in the Appendix.

All of the surviving letters and cards have been printed here complete in chronological sequence. The Appendix contains Adorno's notes and comments on the Arietta theme from Beethoven's Piano Sonata, op. 111, preserved in the Thomas Mann Archive in Zurich, and his notes and sketches for the putative compositions of Adrian Leverkühn mentioned or described in Thomas Mann's novel *Doctor Faustus.*

For the German edition the punctuation and orthography of the originals was generally maintained throughout. A few obvious and insignificant typing errors in the originals have been appropriately corrected without comment for the transcription. Editors' additions have been enclosed in square brackets. Emphases in the original letters, indicated by underlining or spaced print, have been rendered throughout by italics in the transcription. The letterheads and concluding sections of the originals have also been reproduced as closely as possible in the printed text. The passages in Thomas Mann's diary entries which the author underlined in red when preparing the text of *The Story of a Novel: The Genesis of Doctor Faustus* are here also underlined. The brace brackets ({. . .}) in the passage on the 'Apocalipsis' cited in note 10 of Letter 5 enclose words or phrases which Mann included in the published text of *The Story of a Novel*.

The annotations to the letters provide further information concerning the individuals, writings and specific events which are mentioned or alluded to in the correspondence. These annotations are simply intended to clarify certain references and to provide some assistance to the contemporary reader, and do not attempt to supply a detailed running commentary to the correspondence or to provide a substantive contribution to the current state of research on the subject. For this reason, we have not supplied further references to the relevant secondary literature or taken specific account of related correspondence with third parties, such as that between Adorno and Erika Mann for example. It appeared to us more helpful not only to provide specific sources and references for the often detailed discussion of the literary and theoretical writings of the two correspondents, but also to clarify the discussion in question by citation from the relevant writings where appropriate. Similarly we have provided details of Thomas Mann's correspondence with other parties if it serves to illuminate the background and context of his letters to Adorno, as in the case of Thomas Mann's controversy with Arnold Schoenberg.

Information concerning the original textual sources for this edition of the correspondence, and reference to prior publication, in part or whole, of the same material where relevant, has been provided at the end of each letter immediately before the annotations. The following abbreviations have been employed:

O: Original
Ms: Manuscript
Ts: Typescript
Fp: First published
Pp: Part published

The following abbreviations have been employed in the annotations with reference to the writings of Adorno and to the works, diaries and letters of Thomas Mann:

GS [1–20]: Theodor W. Adorno, *Gesammelte Schriften*, ed. Rolf Tiedemann in collaboration with Gretel Adorno, Susan Buck-Morss and Klaus Schultz, vols. 1–20, Frankfurt am Main, 1970–86.

GW [I–XIII]: Thomas Mann: *Gesammelte Werke in dreizehn Bänden*, 2nd edn, Frankfurt am Main, 1974.

Tagebücher: Thomas Mann, *Tagebücher*, ed. Peter de Mendelssohn (*1918–1922; 1931–1943*) and Inge Jens (*1944–1955*), Frankfurt am Main, 1977–95.

Briefe II: Thomas Mann, *Briefe 1937–1947*, ed. Erika Mann, Frankfurt am Main, 1963.

Briefe III: Thomas Mann, *Briefe 1948–1955*, ed. Erika Mann, Frankfurt am Main, 1965.

DüD: *Dichter über ihre Dichtungen*, ed. Rudolf Hirsch and Werner Vordtriede, Vol. 14/III: *Thomas Mann, Teil III: 1944–1955*, ed. Hans Wysling in collaboration with Marianne Fischer, Frankfurt am Main, 1981.

The editors would also like to express their gratitude to the following individuals for their considerable assistance in the course of preparing this edition: Peter Cahn, Michael Maaser, Elisabeth Matthias, Veró van de Sand, Peter Stocker and, at the Thomas Mann Archive, Rosamerie Primault, Katrin Bedenig and Cornelia Bernini.

Correspondence 1943–1955

1   THOMAS MANN TO THEODOR W. ADORNO
    PACIFIC PALISADES, 5.10.1943

THOMAS MANN   1550
                                              SAN REMO DRIVE
                                    PACIFIC PALISADES, CALIFORNIA

                                                    5.X.43

Dear Dr Adorno,
    Once again many thanks for yesterday's splendid evening.[1] Lest it
should get mislaid, I also enclose your article[2] – very stimulating
reading and extremely important for the figure of Kretzschmar who,
in typically musical-historical fashion, had never advanced beyond the
perspective which 'absolutizes the personality';[3] yet he, if anyone,
should be able to appreciate how the proximity of death and greatness
produces a certain objectivism (with a tendency towards the conven-
tional) where the sovereignly subjective passes over into the mythic.
So do not be too surprised if Kretschmar now starts to incorporate
such thoughts into his own perorations![4] I am not worried about
montage in this connection,[5] and never really have been. What belongs
in the book must go into it, and will be properly absorbed in the
process.
    I also wanted to ask if you could write out for me, in very simple
form, the arietta theme of the variation movement,[6] and could identify the particular note that is *added* to the final repetitions and thus
creates the remarkably consoling and humane effect at the close.
    Was it also in the same movement[7] that the melody consists in the
chordal texture rather than in the repeated unchanging upper notes?
And which was the note that was repeated four times over alternating
chords?
    I need this degree of musical intimacy and characteristic detail, and
can only acquire it from a remarkable connoisseur like yourself.
    Heartfelt greetings from both of us,
                            Yours,
                            Thomas Mann

SOURCE: O: MS with printed letterhead; Theodor W. Adorno Archive,
Frankfurt am Main. Fp: *DüD*, p. 15.

1 Thomas Mann and Theodor W. Adorno probably first met one another
in 1942 or 1943 at the home of Max Horkheimer (1895–1973) and his wife,
Maidon (1887–1969), who on settling in California found themselves
living in the vicinity of the Manns. The earliest direct evidence of personal

3

acquaintance is to be found in Adorno's letter to his parents on 29 March 1943: 'This evening at Max's with a couple of celebrities including Thomas Mann accompanied by his gracious wife.' They seem to have got to know one another more closely only after Mann had begun work on his novel *Doctor Faustus* in the summer of 1943. At the beginning of July 1943, when Mann was working on the fourth chapter, Adorno showed him a book by Julius Bahl, *Eingebung und Tat im musikalischen Schaffen* (Leipzig, 1939) [Act and Inspiration in Musical Composition], and this became one of Mann's sources for the novel. But what proved decisive for their very close subsequent collaboration was the first part of Adorno's own *Philosophy of the New Music*, which Mann received in manuscript on 21 July 1943 and read at once (typescript in the Thomas Mann Archive, Zurich). In his diary entry for 26 July Mann writes: 'Just finished Adorno's text. Further reflections on how to proceed with Adrian.' On completing the eighth chapter, in which Adrian Leverkühn attends Wendell Kretzschmar's first two lectures (on Beethoven's last Piano Sonata, op. 111, and on 'Beethoven and the Fugue'), Mann records an 'invitation to Dr Adorno, for whom I should like to recite chapter VIII' (Mann, *Tagebücher 1940–1943*, p. 629). On 27 September he read the entire chapter to Adorno and subsequently took careful note of the latter's critical comments and observations in revising the text. On 4 October Mann was invited to dinner at the Adornos. He noted in his diary: '7.15. Dinner at Adorno's home. After coffee showed the three-page insertion concerning the piano. <u>Playing of Beethoven's sonata op. 111.</u> <u>Parallels in op. 31, 2. Easy piano pieces for Adrian.</u> Much talk of music' (ibid., p. 634). Mann was occupied repeatedly with revisions to chapter 8 until the end of the year. In addition he made use of Adorno's essay 'Beethoven's Late Style', also mentioned in this letter. On 5 January 1944 Adorno was once again invited to dinner at the Manns: 'Afterwards op. 111 played again, with inscription of the performer's name' (*Tagebücher 1944–1946*, p. 5). Kretschmar now scans the motif from the arietta theme of the second movement of op. 111 – as a first expression of thanks for Adorno's assistance – not merely with 'Him-mels-blau' [heav-en's blue] or 'Lie-besleid' [lov-er's pain], as in the original version, but also with 'Wie-sen-grund' [mead-ow-land]. (See Thomas Mann, *Doctor Faustus: The Life of the German Composer Adrian Leverkühn as Told by a Friend*, trans. H. T. Lowe-Porter, Harmondsworth, 1968, ch. 8, p. 56.) There was another meeting between Mann and Adorno, at the home of Berthold (1885–1953) and Salka (1889–1978) Viertel on 23 January 1944, at which 'the musical problematic of the novel' was also discussed. On this occasion Adorno drew Mann's attention to Willi Reich's volume on Alban Berg (Vienna, 1937) to which Adorno had contributed several essays, and which became in turn an important source for the novel. This effectively marks the end of the first phase of their active collaboration. Nonetheless, Thomas Mann's diary records numerous further meetings. And Adorno's texts on Alban Berg, Wagner and Kierkegaard, the beginnings of *Minima Moralia*, and especially the section of the *Philosophy of the New Music*, which was devoted specifically to Schoenberg, continued to accompany Mann's own work on *Doctor Faustus*. They essentially form the basis for the collaboration which was renewed in the winter of 1945–6 and lasted until the completion of Mann's novel (see Letter 5, below), and which constitutes a major theme of the correspondence itself.

2 See Theodor W. Adorno, 'Spätstil Beethovens', *Der Auftakt*, 17 (5/6) (1937), pp. 65–7; *GS* 17, pp. 13–17. English translation: 'Late Style in Beethoven', in T. W. Adorno, *Essays on Music*, ed. Richard Leppert (Berkeley, Los Angeles and London, 2002), pp. 564–6.

3 Thomas Mann is probably alluding to the essay 'Late Style in Beethoven', where Adorno writes: 'The maturity of the late works of significant artists does not resemble that of fruit. They are, for the most part, not rounded, but furrowed, even ravaged. Devoid of sweetness, bitter and spiny, they do not surrender themselves to mere delectation. They lack all the harmony that the classicist aesthetic is accustomed to demanding from works of art, and they show more traces of history than of growth. The standard view explains this with the argument that they are products of an uninhibited subjectivity, or, better yet, of "personality", that breaks through all rounded form for the sake of self-expression, transforming harmony into the dissonance of its own suffering, and disdaining sensuous charms with the sovereign self-assurance of the liberated spirit. The late works are thereby relegated to the margins of art where they come to resemble documents. And indeed discussions of the late Beethoven rarely fail to allude to biography and fate' (*GS* 17, p. 13; English translation: 'Late Style in Beethoven', ibid., p. 564).

4 Wendell Kretschmar's lectures as related in chapter 8 of *Doctor Faustus*, in particular his remarks on 'Beethoven's condition in the year 1820'. See Thomas Mann, *Doktor Faustus*, *GW* VI, pp. 71–4; English translation: *Doctor Faustus*, chapter 8, pp. 53–5.

5 See Mann's further remarks on this subject in Letter 5 below.

6 On 6 October Adorno sent Thomas Mann a handwritten copy of the 'arietta theme' from the second and concluding movement of Beethoven's Piano Sonata, op. 111, with relevant explanatory comments, just as Mann had requested in his letter (see Appendix, pp. 120–1). These materials are preserved in the Thomas Mann Archive.

7 Thomas Mann is probably alluding to the frequent repetition of the 'd' at the beginning of the second movement of op. 111; but it is also possible that he is thinking of the exposition section of the first movement of Sonata op. 31, no. 2, which Adorno had also played for him on the same evening.

THE LIBRARY OF CONGRESS   WASHINGTON
THE CONSULTANT IN GERMANIC LITERATURE

Pacif. Palisades, 27.IX.44

Dear Dr Adorno,

I have been sent the enclosed lecture by Dr Albersheim[1] which I have
read with cautious interest. It made a strong impression at the Music
Congress, and they are saying it will earn the author a chair in music-
ology. You will understand that I should be extraordinarily interested
to hear your own opinion upon the matter (and I do not mean concerning the chair).

I am studying your work on Wagner[2] before embarking on
the 'Fragments'.[3] The section on phantasmagoria, 'semblance' and
'diminution' is what has most delighted me so far.[4] Lohengrin as a tiny
fairy prince (with the pianissimo trumpet representing the horn) is
wonderful.[5]

Yours,
Thomas Mann

SOURCE: O: MS with printed letterhead; Theodor W. Adorno Archive,
Frankfurt am Main. Pp: *DüD*, p. 29.

1 Alfred Neumann (1895–1952) had sent Thomas Mann a lecture by the
Viennese pianist and musicologist Gerhard Albersheim (1902–1996), entitled
'Contemporary Music in the Light of the History of Musical Art'. Albersheim,
who had emigrated in 1939, had been teaching at the University of Southern
California since 1940. It was there that he delivered the lecture in question, on
15 September at the Institute of Contemporary Music. Nothing further is
known of the 'Music Congress' mentioned in the letter. A copy of the lecture
is included among the preparatory materials for *Doctor Faustus* in the Thomas
Mann Archive in Munich.

2 Four chapters of Adorno's book on Wagner (the first, the sixth and the last
two) had already appeared in 1939 under the title 'Fragments on Wagner', in
the *Zeitschrift für Sozialforschung*, 8 (1939), pp. 1–49; the book edition of
Adorno's *Versuch über Wagner*, written in London and New York in 1938–9,
appeared only in 1952 (*GS* 13, pp. 7–148); English translation: *In Search of
Wagner*, trans. R. Livingstone (London and New York, 1991).

3 See Max Horkheimer and Theodor W. Adorno, *Philosophische Fragmente*,
New York: Institute of Social Research, 1944. This was the original

mimeograph version of the authors' *Dialectic of Enlightenment*; the first book edition appeared in 1947, published by Querido Verlag of Amsterdam; now in *GS* 3, pp. 7–296.

4 Mann is referring to the beginning of the sixth chapter of Adorno's *Versuch über Wagner* (entitled 'Phantasmagoria'); see *GS* 13, p. 82f.; English translation: *In Search of Wagner*, p. 85f.

5 'The technique of diminishing the sound by eliminating the bass also confers the quality of phantasmagoria on a passage in *Lohengrin*, one which, less obviously than in *Tristan*, determines the character of the whole work. It is Elsa's vision in which she conjures up the knight and thus launches the entire action. Her description of the knight resembles the picture of Oberon: the inward Lohengrin is a tiny fairy prince. "Arrayed in shining armour a knight was approaching, more virtuous and pure than any I had yet seen, a golden horn at his hip and leaning on his sword. Thus was this worthy knight sent to me from heaven" [*Lohengrin*, act 1, scene 1]. Such bass notes as occur are given once more to ethereal instruments such as the bass clarinets or the harp. The sound of the bass clarinets, which is particularly transparent, never descends below middle c. The horn referred to in the text is envisaged as a diminished scale in the music by a trumpet in pianissimo' (*GS* 13, p. 83; English translation: *In Search of Wagner*, pp. 86–7).

3 THOMAS MANN TO THEODOR W. ADORNO
    PACIFIC PALISADES, 13.12.1944

THE LIBRARY OF CONGRESS   WASHINGTON
THE CONSULTANT IN GERMANIC LITERATURE

                                            Pacif. Palisades, 13 Dec. 44

My dear Dr Adorno,
    Here is the letter[1] which I am about to despatch to President KleinSmid. I hope I have done it properly, and I think he may wish to get in touch with me personally about the matter. But he will certainly be able to make some enquiries in the relevant musical circles.
    I must also thank you for the essay on 'Spengler Today',[2] an extremely perceptive and well-informed piece of work – like everything else you write. The often silly parody of Nietzsche and the infantile romanticism that is always so ready to glorify beasts of prey could perhaps be brought out even more strongly. But your critique is very just. You have evoked everything really well: what is both captivating and repellent about him, what looks so attractive and traditional at first

7

sight, the Goethe, the Schopenhauer, but also the aspect of the threat-
ening School Master.

Respectfully yours,
Thomas Mann

SOURCE: O: MS with printed letterhead; Theodor W. Adorno Archive,
Frankfurt am Main.

1 Adorno had asked Thomas Mann if he would write a letter of recommendation for Eduard Steuermann (see Letter 11, note 9). It had become clear that
the University of Southern California was intending to expand its 'musical
department' and that Steuermann might therefore be able to obtain a teaching position there. On 13 December Thomas Mann wrote, in English, to
Rufus Bernard von KleinSmid (1875–1964), who was president of the university between 1921 and 1947:

Dear Mr President:

You can hardly believe how interested I, as an old music lover, was in
the news of the intended considerable enlargement of the musical department of your university. This is a change of great importance for the cultural and especially the musical life of this coast. That such plans can be
conceived and executed during a great war, demanding all the energies of
the nation, is a proof of the vitality of this country of which I am now a
citizen.

Please take it as a sign of my deep interest if I want to direct your attention to a man who, in my opinion, would be a real asset to the newly
enlarged institute. I am speaking of the pianist Eduard Steuermann, a
musician of the first order, who combines an extraordinary productive
and reproductive gift with a decided and proven pedagogical talent. His
great ability, and especially his educational prowess, were early recognized in Europe, and he was offered a professorship at the Vienna
Academy which, however, he refused in order to go to America.

A pupil of Busoni and later of Arnold Schoenberg, Steuermann belongs
to a modern and even radically modern generation and school of musicians. Perhaps in music, more than in any other art, radical progressive-
ness may be combined with the most devoted and faithful loyalty to the
old and classical tradition, in the same way, Steuermann is an artist of the
profoundest and most thorough classical education, and as a teacher
makes this also a prerequisite for any progressive venture. He is known
as the editor of the best edition of Brahms' piano pieces, with which he
was commissioned by the Universal Edition. He is not only one of the best
known interpreters of modern music, but also of Beethoven and Brahms
piano compositions.

I am telling you all this, dear Mr President, because I know that, although
in Europe this artist would have an assured and brilliant career ahead of
him, Steuermann is not the man to push and cleverly recommend himself. I
hardly believe that he will approach you of his own volition in order to
apply for a position with your future institute. And this is the reason why I

8

give you all these data which you can easily verify and complete through an inquiry in musical circles. I would not have written to you if I did not believe to be serving the university as well as a great artist with these lines.

Steuermann, who had been living in New York since 1937, and whose sister Salka Viertel had made her home in Santa Monica into something of a social focus for the emigrant community, did not move to California after all.

2 Mann is referring to an essay which Adorno originally presented as a lecture in 1937, but which was published in 1941 in *Studies in Philosophy and Social Science* (IX, 2, pp. 305–25). (After the outbreak of war the *Zeitschrift für Sozialforschung* was published in New York under this English title.) See 'Spengler nach dem Untergang', now in *GS* 10.1, pp. 47–71; for the passages to which Mann alludes specifically, see esp. pp. 52f., 62f. and 69. (English translation: 'Spengler after the Decline', in *Prisms*, trans. Samuel Weber and Shierry Weber (London, 1969), pp. 57f., 64f. and 70.)

4 THEODOR W. ADORNO TO THOMAS MANN
   LOS ANGELES, 3.6.1945

3 June 1945

316 So. Kenter Ave.
Los Angeles 24.

My dear and esteemed Dr Mann,
   I feel the most profound need to impart to you all of my best wishes and fairest hopes for your seventieth birthday.[1] This moment, which finds you as it does completely absorbed in uninterrupted work and self-forgetful productivity, has crept up upon us with such stealth that it is hard to believe how many years have passed already and it seems improper even to allude to them. It is as if such congratulations, inevitably implying a sort of caesura, might wrongly disturb the unfolding course of your spiritual experience, an experience that regards nothing as alien to itself, tolerates nothing imposed upon it from without, and expresses what is most human about us through a kind of *mémoire involontaire*.[2] But you will forgive me if an observer may permit himself something which your silent and tireless work so strenuously denies itself – pausing here, therefore, to give thanks and to express the hope that this caesura remains imperceptible to you, especially as this current celebration of your seventieth birthday cannot fail to strike anyone remotely familiar with your writings as anything other than a kind of subtle, wary and ironic artistic device in its own right. Who after all, one might ask, has ever stayed more faithful to the utopia of youth, to the dream of a world unspoilt by ends and purposes, for all your

unremitting emphasis upon maturity and responsibility? Can your entire oeuvre be described as anything but a unique fusion of the early and the late, as a single determinate negation of the normal and average life that lies between the two? Is not even this your seventieth birthday the authentic counterpoint to little Hanno's evening at the opera?[3] I know that I can only give full expression to my personal gratitude by confessing that the resonance of your words and the character of your imaginative creations impressed themselves so strongly upon me during the years in which I ceased to be a child that I could no longer begin to separate these impressions from the loves and friendships belonging to those years. You have addressed the life which precedes all art, and thereby vouchsafed the fundamental experience of art itself. This spiritual and biological proximity itself complements something else that has also touched me very deeply. When I was able to meet you here in person, upon this remote western coast, I had the feeling that I was only now, for the first time, actually encountering that German tradition from which I have received everything – including the strength to resist the tradition. This feeling, together with the happiness it grants – a theologian would speak here of a blessing – is something that I shall never forget. There was one occasion – it was in Kampen in the summer of 1921[4] – when I followed on behind you for a good way, unnoticed, as you walked, and imagined what it would be like if you were to turn and speak to me. That you have indeed truly spoken to me now, after twenty years, is a moment of realized utopia that is rarely vouchsafed to any human being.

I had wished to honour this caesura with a couple of new little songs,[5] but in the event my troubled brain has not allowed me to do so. Hopefully I shall make good this omission in future. Much closer to my heart today is simply this – that your grief for the wretched state of the world shall not deter the joyful completion of your own work on Leverkühn, something of which I wait impatiently to hear.

With the profoundest respect,
Yours, T. W. Adorno

SOURCE: O: MS; Thomas Mann Archive, Zurich. Fp: *Frankfurter Adorno Blätter* I (1992), p. 28f.

1 Thomas Mann celebrated his birthday in New York on 6 June 1945.

2 The phenomenon of spontaneous and unbidden memory as described in the work of Marcel Proust (1871–1922), whose ideas were strongly influenced here by Henri Bergson (1859–1941).

3 Adorno is alluding to the performance of *Fidelio*, mentioned in chapter 8 of part VIII, not that of *Lohengrin*, referred to in chapter 2 of part XI, in Thomas

Mann's novel *Buddenbrooks*. English translation: *Buddenbrooks: The Decline of a Family*, trans. by H. T. Lowe-Porter (Harmondsworth, 1957), p. 405f.

4 During a summer trip between 7 August and 13 September 1921, Thomas Mann spent some time in Sylt (23–31 August). Nothing further is known about Adorno's stay in Kampen that is documented for the period between the end of August and the beginning of September 1921.

5 In fact Adorno composed no more songs after completing the Four Songs to Texts by Stefan George, op. 7, in 1944.

5 THOMAS MANN TO THEODOR W. ADORNO
   PACIFIC PALISADES, 30/31.12.1945

THOMAS MANN   1550
                                              SAN REMO DRIVE
                                    PACIFIC PALISADES, CALIFORNIA

                                                     30 Dec. 1945

Dear Dr Adorno,
    I should just like to say something about the manuscript I recently left with you and which I imagine you may be about to read.[1] In writing to you I certainly do not feel I am interrupting my work in any way.
    I am quite excited that this strange and perhaps impossible work (what there is of it) is in your hands. For in the states of weariness which increasingly assail me I often wonder whether I should not abandon the whole thing, and your own view of the matter will not be without influence upon whether I persevere or not.
    The aspect with regard to which I should principally be grateful to receive some detailed comment is the principle of *montage* which peculiarly, perhaps outrageously, pervades the entire book – explicitly so and without the slightest concealment. Only recently I have been struck by this again in a half amusing, half uncanny fashion when I came to describe a critical illness in the life of my hero. For I incorporated Nietzsche's actual symptoms[2] word for word, just as they are described in his letters, along with details of his prescribed diet etc., straight into the book. I simply pasted them in, so to speak, for anyone to recognize. I have followed the same principle with the motif of Tchaikovsky's invisible admirer and lover, Madame von Meck, whom he never met, indeed expressly avoided meeting in the flesh.[3] I paste this familiar historical material in and allow the edges to blur, dropping it into the text as a mythical theme there for anyone to pick up. (For Leverkühn the relationship is a way of circumventing the devil's proscription of love, the commandment enjoining coldness.)

11

Or to take another example – towards the end of the book I obviously introduce the theme, complete with actual quotations, from Shakespeare's sonnets: the triangle where the friend sends his friend to woo the beloved on his behalf – and the friend ends up 'wooing for himself'.[4] Of course, I also transform the material: Adrian *kills* the friend whom he loves since the resulting involvement with the woman in question exposes him in the end to an act of murderous jealousy (Innes Rodde). Nonetheless, this does little to alter the bold and thievish character of my borrowings.

It hardly seems sufficient to plead Molière's 'Je prends mon bien où je le trouve'[5] as a justification for such conduct. Perhaps it springs from an inclination as one becomes *older* to regard life as a cultural product, preferring in one's petrified dignity to interpret it through mythical cliché rather than 'independent' invention. But I am only too aware that I have long practised this kind of higher transcription – as in the description of little Hanno Buddenbrook's typhoid fever, when I unabashedly transcribed the relevant article from an encyclopaedia[6] and subsequently 'versified' it so to speak. This chapter has become rather famous. Yet its merit derives solely from a spiritual and creative elaboration of mechanically appropriated material (and the trick of indirectly communicating the fact of Hanno's death).

The case is more difficult, not to say more scandalous, when it is a question of appropriating material which *is itself already spirit*, that is, of an authentically literary borrowing, and performed with an air that what has been filched in this way is just good enough to serve one's own compositional purposes. You will rightly gather that I am thinking here of the brazen – although I hope not too doltish – way in which I have raided parts of your writings on the philosophy of music.[7] And I owe you a particular apology precisely because at present the reader can hardly be made aware of these borrowings unless I find a way of acknowledging them without ruining the artistic illusion (a footnote like: 'This derives from Adorno-Wiesengrund'? That surely won't do). It is curious: my own relationship to music has been fairly widely recognized, I have always been adept at literary music-making, I have always felt halfway to being a musician myself, and I have tried to transfer the musical technique of interweaving motifs to the structure of the novel. And only recently, for instance, Ernst Toch expressly and emphatically congratulated me for being 'musically initiated'.[8] But to write a novel about a musician, a novel that at times even aspires to become, among other things, and along with other things, a novel about music itself – this demands more than mere 'initiation'. It requires a *scholarship* that I simply do not possess. Hence I was determined from the start, in a book already beholden to the principle of montage, not to shrink from seeking assistance or support from the specialist work of others – in the confidence that what has been gleaned and learned from other people may nonetheless take on an independent function and symbolic life of its own within the literary composition – yet *still remain intact* in the works of criticism from which it derives.

My hope is that you will also share this view. The fact is that my own musical education scarcely extends beyond the late romantics, and you have given me an idea of the most modern developments in music, which is just what I require for a book which again, among other things, and together with many other things, takes the *predicament of art* as its subject. As in the earlier case of little Hanno's typhoid fever, my 'initiated' ignorance required precise *details* to enhance the literary illusion and structure of the composition. And I would be deeply obliged if you would intervene and correct such details (which I have not derived entirely from you) if they should appear mistaken, misleading, or expressed in such a way as to provoke the scorn of experts. *One* passage has already been subjected to expert judgement. I read the passages on opus 111 to Bruno Walter and he was *delighted*.[9] 'Well, this is magnificent. Nothing better has ever been said about Beethoven! I had no idea that you had delved so deeply into the composer!' Nonetheless, I have no wish to set up the expert as the sole judge here. The musical expert in particular, always proud of his arcane knowledge, is for my purposes all too ready to betray a condescending smile. I would cautiously suggest, *cum grano salis*, that something may produce the right effect, may come out sounding right, without being entirely so. – But I am not attempting to ingratiate myself with you.

I have brought the novel to the point where Leverkühn, at the age of thirty-five, in a first wave of euphoric inspiration, and in an incredibly short period of time, composes his principal work, or at least his first principal work, the *Apocalypsis cum figuris*,[10] based upon the fifteen illustrations of Dürer or perhaps directly upon the text of the *Book of Revelation*. And my task now is to imagine and characterize the work in the most suggestive possible manner (a work that I think of as a very *German* creation, as an oratorio with orchestra, choruses, soloists, and narrator). And I am basically writing this letter in order to clarify for my mind's eye something that as yet I have hardly dared to approach. What I need are some significant and characteristic *details* (only a few are required) which will create a plausible, indeed convincing, picture for the reader. Would you consider, with me, how such a work – and I mean Leverkühn's work – could more or less be practically realized, and how you would compose the music if you yourself were in league with the devil? And could you suggest one or two musical features to further the imaginative illusion? – What I have in mind is something satanically religious and demonically devout, at once rigorously traditional and violently transgressive, something that often seems to scorn the idea of art itself, that reaches right back to the primitive and the elemental (as in Kretzschmar's reminiscences of Beissel),[11] that abandons regular metre or even tonality (trombone glissandi); and perhaps also something that is scarcely performable: like ancient church modes or non-tempered a capella choruses with notes and intervals one would hardly find on the keyboard etc. But of course it is very easy to say 'etc.'

Even as I was writing these lines I have learned that I shall be seeing you earlier than I thought since a meeting has already been arranged for Wednesday afternoon. So I could have said all this to you in person after all! But it still seems fitting, and I am thereby relieved, that you now have it written down in black and white. Let it be the basis for our ensuing discussion, as well as a record for posterity, if there should be a posterity.

Yours faithfully,
Thomas Mann

SOURCE: O: MS with printed letterhead; Theodor W. Adorno Archive, Frankfurt am Main. Fp: *Briefe III*, p. 469ff.

1 Thomas Mann had presented Adorno with a copy of the manuscript of his Dr Faustus novel (as far as chapter 33) on 5 December 1945. The entry in Mann's diary for this date reads: 'After dinner to Adorno's, handed over the manuscript of my novel for subsequent musical and creative advice once he has had an opportunity to ponder its contents' (*Tagebücher 1944–1946*, p. 282). On 28 December 1945 Mann notes in his diary: 'Learned that Adorno has read the ms. and made notes for further discussion' (ibid., p. 290).

2 See Friedrich Nietzsche's letters from June and July 1875 (to his mother, his sister, Erwin Rohde, Carl von Gerstorf, Franz Overbeck and Marie Baumgartner). Mann used these as source material for chapter 33 of *Doctor Faustus*.

3 Nadezhda von Meck was a patron of Tchaikovsky. She played a significant role in the composer's life, although they never met in person.

4 See *Doctor Faustus*, chapters 41–2. For the theme of the friend as suitor in Shakespeare, see esp. sonnets 40, 41 and 42.

5 The expression derives from Molière's reply to the charge of using material from Cyrano de Bergerac's play *Le Pédant Joué* as the basis for a couple of scenes in his own piece *Fourberies de Scapin*: 'Il m'est permis de reprendre mon bien où je le trouve'. The remark was commonly repeated, and 'prendre' eventually came to replace the original 'reprendre'.

6 Thomas Mann had specifically consulted the *Brockhaus-Konversationslexikon*, published in 16 volumes (Leipzig, 1895).

7 Thomas Mann is referring to the essay 'Beethoven's Late Style', on which he had drawn for Kretschmar's lectures on Beethoven as described in chapter 8 of *Doctor Faustus*, to the writings on Wagner and to the monograph on Berg, as well as to the typescript of the section of the *Philosophy of the New Music* that was specifically concerned with Schoenberg. The material on Schoenberg had proved crucial for Adrian Leverkühn's dialogue with the devil in chapter 25 of the novel (see the notes to Letters 1 and 2 above). But Thomas Mann had also repeatedly consulted Adorno's study on Kierkegaard in this connection.

8 See Ernst Toch, 'Thomas Mann und die Musik', in *Die neue Rundschau, Sonderausgabe zu Thomas Manns 70. Geburtstag* (Stockholm, 1945), pp. 187–8. Mann is alluding to the following observation by Toch: '[Mann's] conception of musical experience, both as an imaginative totality and in its intrinsic character, reveals every sign of an initiated musical understanding and the musician can only be delighted by the literary expression which such understanding finds here' (ibid., p. 188; see Thomas Mann, *Tagebücher 1944–1946*, p. 226).

9 The conductor Bruno Walter (1876–1962), who had been friendly with the Mann family ever since their years in Munich, had written to Katia Mann on 25 December 1945: 'I cannot describe what a powerful and uplifting impression the Beethoven chapter from Dr Faustus has exerted upon me. Nothing remotely as profound and illuminating as this has ever been said about Beethoven before' (Bruno Walter, *Briefe 1894–1962*, ed. Lotte Walter-Lind, Frankfurt am Main, 1969, p. 280).

10 In his *Story of a Novel* (see Letter 9, note 1) Thomas Mann described the beginning of his collaboration with Adorno on the *Apocalipsis cum figuris* as follows: 'Adorno did not yet have any musical instructions and directions for Leverkühn's opus which he could give me, but he assured me that he was thinking about the matter, that he already had all sorts of ideas stirring inside him, and that he would shortly be ready to assist me. Not to relate the way in which he kept his word would be to leave these memoirs very incomplete. During the weeks to come I sat with him many a time with notebook and pencil, over a good home-brewed fruit liqueur, jotting down cue phrases concerning the corrections and more exact details for earlier accounts of works of music in the book, as well as traits he had conceived for the oratorio. Fully cognizant as he was of the intentions of the whole and of this particular section, he aimed his suggestions and recommendations precisely at the essential point, namely, to make the opus open simultaneously to the criticism of bloody barbarism and to the criticism of bloodless intellectualism' (*Die Entstehung des Doktor Faustus: Roman eines Romans*, GW XI, p. 249; English translation: *The Story of a Novel: The Genesis of Doctor Faustus*, trans. Richard Winston and Clara Winston, New York, 1961, p. 125–6). Although Adorno provided Mann with detailed written comments on Leverkühn's Violin Concerto, the Concertante Music for three violins, three winds and piano, and the String Quartet, as well as on the cantata *Dr Fausti Weheklag* (see Appendix, pp. 119ff. and 124ff.), nothing similar has survived

in relation to the *Apocalypsis cum figuris*. But one passage which Mann later deleted from the original text of *The Story of a Novel* gives a fairly precise idea of the 'practically effective and characteristic details' which Adorno had explicitly suggested in this connection (the brace brackets enclose phrases which Mann did include in the published text):

{thoroughly familiar with the intentions of the whole book and those connected with this particular section} which were essentially concerned with {exposing the work to the twin charges of bloody barbarism and bloodless intellectualism} he made some excellent suggestions – with the choral parts moving from whispered sounds, half-sung declamation and mingled speaking voices to the richest expression of vocal polyphony, and the orchestral part passing from a magical and primitive kind of noise to the most developed possible form of musical composition.

Or with gradual transitions of timbre between the vocal and instrumental parts, 'dissolving the boundaries between the human and the thing-like', the idea of entrusting the role of the Babylonian whore to a particularly lovely coloratura soprano voice whose 'virtuoso vocal leaps pass over imperceptibly, with a kind of flute-like effect, into the orchestral sound itself', and of lending certain instruments, on the other hand, the effect and timbre of some grotesque *vox humana*. The suggestion that the most dissonant parts of this despairing piece should express all that is elevated and spiritual, whereas the tonal and harmonic parts should represent the world of hell, i.e. of the intrinsically banal, is authentically Schoenbergian or, better, Bergian in character. From Adrian's melancholic tendency towards parody he developed the demonic merry-go-round, the derisive imitation of every possible musical style, from the motif of the little mermaid the words that beg for a 'soul', from the combination of 'imperial pomp' and musical radicalism the notion of 'explosive archaism'. That could all just as well have come from me, did come from me, like the expression 'the latest reports of the end of the world' which is applied to the chilling high-tenor role of the *testis* – and my advisor suggested all of this through a kind of collaborative imaginative empathy with what I was trying to do. The most significant and useful tip he gave me concerned the effective identity between the sounds of infernal laughter and the angelic children's choir, an exciting moment which I held back for the end of the chapter. Once I was back home I would 'fix' the things that spontaneously came up in discussion, that is, write them out in greater detail – and all I subsequently needed to do was to give the material some compositional order, to articulate its contours, to versify it so to speak, that is: to let the good Serenus relate all this directly from the heart, breathing deeply and heavily as he gives voice to feelings of love and horror. (Thomas Mann, TS pp. 140–1; MS pp. 120–1) (See *Tagebücher 1946–1948*, p. 950f.).

Mann's diary for 1946 records such working discussions on 3, 6, 13 and 20 January, and further meetings on 16 and 20 February. On 2 March Mann's entry reads: 'Oratorio completed. Corrections begun' (*Tagebücher 1944–1946*, p. 311). Following his operation (see Letter 6 below), Mann resumed work on *Doctor Faustus* on 30 May 1946. The diary subsequently records a meeting with Adorno on 4 July, and eight further meetings are recorded before the end of November, when Mann begins working on the account of Leverkühn's cantata *Doktor Fausti Weheklag*. On 25 November Mann notes: '<u>Discussion with Adorno on the "Symphonic Cantata"</u>' (*Tagebücher 1946–1948*, p. 67). The collaboration once again became particularly intensive during the last couple of months before actual completion of the novel. Mann revisited and revised his descriptions of Leverkühn's Chamber Music and Violin Concerto in accordance with Adorno's sketches and proposals.

11 Wendell Kretzschmar's fourth lecture in chapter 8 of *Doctor Faustus* (see *GW* VI, pp. 86–93; English translation: pp. 65–8).

6 THOMAS MANN TO GRETEL AND THEODOR W. ADORNO
   CHICAGO, 19.5.1946

Chicago

19.V.1946

Dear Friends, heartfelt greetings before we meet again! I must say that I am feeling unjustifiably well under the circumstances;[1] and I shall simply have to cope with shortness of breath for a while – though God certainly created me with long breath in the first place. We are thinking of leaving on the 24th and look forward to finding you both in the best of health.

Yours, Thomas Mann

SOURCE: Postcard: Clinic Group – the University of Chicago; Postmark: Chicago, Ill., May 21, 1946. O: MS; Theodor W. Adorno Archive, Frankfurt am Main. Fp: *Briefe II*, p. 489.

1 In the middle of April 1946 Thomas Mann had been obliged to go into hospital for a lung operation. He remained in Billings Hospital, Chicago, until 25 May 1946.

THOMAS MANN   1550
                                          SAN REMO DRIVE
                            PACIFIC PALISADES, CALIFORNIA

                                                 8 Nov. 1947

Dear Dr Adorno,

I just wanted to send you this Swiss review of *Faustus* on account
of the passage I have specifically marked.[1] There have been other more
dramatic notices, but the impression that the music itself is so central,
and the convincing character of the biographical fiction in general, is
particularly important to me.

The *Neue Zürcher Zeitung* has also printed an announcement,[2]
albeit a rather breathless one, that they will be publishing a musician's discussion of the book,[3] specifically naming the music critic
Dr Schuh[4] in this connection: we can only be curious to see what he
says!

With very best wishes
T. M.

PS I would be grateful if you could return the piece in due course.

SOURCE: O: MS with printed letterhead; Theodor W. Adorno Archive,
Frankfurt am Main. Fp: *Briefe II*, p. 567.

---

1 The first European edition of *Doctor Faustus* had appeared on 17 October.
Thomas Mann's diary entry for 8 November 1947 reveals that he is referring
here to a review of the novel by Alexander Moritz Frey (1881–1957) which
was published in the Basel *National-Zeitung* on 2 November 1947 (p. 8). The
review, which Mann received on 6 November, emphasizes the 'convincingly
real character of the music' described in the novel (*Tagebücher 1946–1948*,
p. 180). Frey expatiated on this aspect: 'The author communicates in musical
terms – in genuinely musical terms precisely as a composer conceives them –
the ultimate sense of the world in all its celestial heights and infernal depths.
His knowledge of the work and workshop of the composer is so profound,
his digressions on the secret mysteries of creative musical achievement are so
detailed, that one can hardly avoid the uplifting but also disturbing impression that there must be an actual musical work like that described in *Doctor
Faustus* itself – and this because Thomas Mann has effectively created and
bestowed the most precise form upon this idea through the very power of his
language. No professional musician can fail to acknowledge and to be
inspired by this dimension of Mann's imposing novel.' The copy of the review
which is preserved in the Thomas Mann Archive has not been marked in any

18

way, but this is probably the passage to which Mann specifically intended to draw Adorno's attention.

2 See E[duard] K[orrodi], 'Thomas Manns "Doktor Faustus"', *Neue Zürcher Zeitung*, 22 October 1947, p. 6.

3 See E[duard] K[orrodi], Ernst Hadorn and Willi Schuh, 'Thomas Manns "Doktor Faustus"', *Neue Zürcher Zeitung*, 29 November and 6 December 1947, p. 5 and p. 7.

4 Willi Schuh (1900–1986), who had studied music in Munich between 1922 and 1924, had been the music critic (from 1928) and the music editor (from 1944) with the *Neue Zürcher Zeitung*. He taught the theory of harmony and the history of music at the Zurich Conservatory and was particularly active in promoting the cause of contemporary music. Schuh also edited the *Schweizerische Musikzeitung* between 1941 and 1968. He published a monograph, *Richard Strauss. Betrachtungen und Erinnerungen* [Richard Strauss: Reflections and Reminiscences] in Zurich in 1949. Schuh had already expressed public support for Thomas Mann on the occasion of the 'Protest of Munich, City of Richard Wagner' in 1933. Mann never forgot this earlier act of solidarity and continued to remain in regular contact with Schuh. He mentions him explicitly in chapter 39 of *Doctor Faustus* as 'Dr Schuh, the excellent music-critic of the *Neue Zürcher Zeitung*' (English translation: Harmondsworth, 1968, p. 402).

8   THOMAS MANN TO THEODOR W. ADORNO
PACIFIC PALISADES, 18.12.1947

THOMAS MANN   1550
SAN REMO DRIVE
PACIFIC PALISADES, CALIFORNIA

18 Dec. 1947.

Dear Dr Adorno,

I feel bound to tell you a little more about the symposium[1] which has now appeared over a couple of issues of the *Neue Zürcher Zeitung*, and in particular certain complimentary remarks by Dr Schuh[2] which I ought by rights to *pass on to you*. My only service is to have found a home for good things and instilled them into the soul of the composition.

I must say that the literary circles in Switzerland have become quite excited in this connection. The idea of such a colloquium is surely unique in the history of the journalistic book review.

We don't get to see each other nearly as often as we should. And now of course there are children and grandchildren, busy reunions

19

and celebrations of one kind or another. Once Christmas has passed we must really find time for a quiet evening of conversation again.

Greetings from one household to another!

Yours, T. M.

SOURCE: O: MS with printed letterhead; Theodor W. Adorno Archive, Frankfurt am Main. Fp: *Briefe II*, p. 577.

1 See the note to Letter 7 above.

2 Willi Schuh's contribution to the *Neue Zürcher Zeitung* on 6 December 1947 concentrates upon the question of Leverkühn's musical development. In one passage Schuh writes as follows: 'In the works of his final period, he [i.e. Adrian Leverkühn] succeeds in that ultimate ambition which led him to conclude his pact with the infernal powers in the first place, namely the "reconstruction of expression, the highest and deepest appeal to feeling", but now accomplished on the highest possible level of spiritual insight and formal-technical rigour. In the *Apocalipsis cum figuris* and *Fausti Weheklag* – and the intimately detailed descriptions of these pieces are quite breathtaking for anyone who is truly familiar with the art of music – the composer abandons himself entirely to his work without worrying about any pre-given subjective construction (i.e. a specific twelve-tone row). [. . .] Thomas Mann illuminates the predicament of modern music and its fundamental problem, and does so right down to the most specific technical and material issues involved, in an extremely confident and sure-footed way that derives from a profound knowledge of music and a truly living sympathy with its fortunes. The discussion of particular details – like specific modulations and other harmonic peculiarities, and most especially the details of twelve-tone technique – addresses some of the most sophisticated aspects of music which are unfamiliar even to many musicians. For example, the author not only describes in detail the constructive principles behind Schönberg's dodecaphonic technique, – and *Fausti Weheklag* is explicitly based upon a quite specific tone row, one which embraces all the intervals – but also makes a contribution to some of the most burning contemporary problems in this field: like that of "reconstructing previously used material through the process of constellation", i.e. that of incorporating tonal elements within an atonal system [. . .].'

THOMAS MANN   1550
                                              SAN REMO DRIVE
                                  PACIFIC PALISADES, CALIFORNIA

                                                 2 July 1948

Dear Dr Adorno,
    I have now begun work on the autobiographical memoir concern-
ing the genesis of *Faustus*, or 'The Story of a Novel',[1] and I should be
particularly grateful in this regard if you could furnish me with a few
dates and details about yourself to refresh my memory, about your
origins and the course of your previous life. Perhaps you could say
something more about the – dual Genoese and Viennese? – background of your family, about your musicological and sociological
studies, your relationship with Horckheimer,[2] your earlier academic
career in Frankfurt. – Just a few remarks would be sufficient if that is
all right.
                        Yours,
                        Thomas Mann

SOURCE: O: MS with printed letterhead; Theodor W. Adorno Archive,
Frankfurt am Main. Fp: *DüD*, p. 436.

1 See Thomas Mann, *Die Entstehung des Doktor Faustus: Roman eines
Romans* (Amsterdam, 1949); English translation: *The Story of a Novel: The
Genesis of Doctor Faustus*, trans. Richard Winston and Clara Winston (New
York, 1961). Thomas Mann composed this text between 28 June and 20
September 1948. As early as 13 February 1948 he made the following entry
in his diary: 'Talked to Adorno about my intention to write something auto-
biographical one day concerning *Faustus* – much to his relief' (*Tagebücher
1946–1948*, p. 223).

2 This is how Mann spelt Horkheimer's name in the letter, a mistake which
Walter Benjamin also occasionally made. The philosopher Max Horkheimer
(1895–1973), whom Adorno first met in 1922 at the home of his academic
supervisor Hans Cornelius (1863–1947), qualified as a university teacher in
1925 (with a dissertation on Kant's *Critique of Judgement*) and became professor of social philosophy and director of the Institute for Social Research at
the University of Frankfurt in 1930. Under the auspices of the institute he also
edited the *Zeitschrift für Sozialforschung* from 1932 until 1941. He published
a number of important programmatic essays on the concept of 'critical
theory' in the pages of the *Zeitschrift* during this period. Horkheimer opened
subsidiary branches of the institute in London and Geneva by as early as 1931

and began to rent a personal apartment in Geneva in 1932. After the Nazis forced the closure of the Institute for Social Research in Frankfurt in March 1933, he emigrated with the intention of re-establishing the institute, first of all in Geneva and from 1934 in New York. Horkheimer moved to California in 1941 and settled down with his wife, Maidon, in Pacific Palisades, not far from the Mann family. The Horkheimers, naturalized in 1940, also acted as witnesses for Thomas and Katia Mann when they too became American citizens. Between 1939 and 1944 Horkheimer collaborated with Adorno on the *Dialectic of Enlightenment*. After the war Horkheimer returned to Germany and succeeded in re-establishing the Institute for Social Research in Frankfurt in 1950. From 1951 to 1953 he served as rector of the University of Frankfurt, which had already offered to restore his former chair in 1946. Horkheimer retired in 1959 and died in Nuremberg on 7 July 1973.

10 THOMAS MANN TO THEODOR W. ADORNO
PACIFIC PALISADES, 3.7.1948

THOMAS MANN   1550
SAN REMO DRIVE
PACIFIC PALISADES, CALIFORNIA

3 July 48

Dear Dr Adorno,
Could you say a word – and a positive one if at all possible – about these musical communications?[1] I have just received them from a young Swiss composer by the name of Albert Moeschinger.
I also enclose the reply from Mohr[2] which I forgot to bring with me recently.
Until we meet again soon,
Yours,
T. M.

SOURCE: O: MS with printed letterhead; Theodor W. Adorno Archive, Frankfurt am Main.

1 On 11 July 1948 Thomas Mann received a letter from the Swiss composer Albert Moeschinger (1897–1985), with whom he had already corresponded on the subject of his novel. See 'Albert Moeschingers Briefwechsel mit Thomas Mann', *Schweizer Musikzeitung*, 112/1 (1972), pp. 3–11. In the letter Moeschinger had enclosed his own song setting of Goethe's poem 'Einsamkeit' [Solitude] and a work for piano entitled Four Five-Note Pieces on B–E–A–E–E♭ (in Memory of Adrian Leverkühn). The autograph manuscripts of both pieces are preserved in the Thomas Mann Archive. In *Doctor Faustus* this specific series of notes – the Hetaera–Esmeralda motif – represents Leverkühn's 'infec-

22

tion' and his pact with the Devil and recurs frequently in the composer's works as they are described in the novel.

Albert Moeschinger lived and worked in Bern, as a pianist and teacher at the conservatory, between 1925 and 1943. He later took up residence in Ascona. In addition to a number of symphonies and piano concertos he composed a dramatic cantata for soloists, choir and orchestra, *Die kleine Seejungfrau* [*The Little Mermaid*], op. 75 (1948), which received its first performance with Studio Basel in 1949. It is not known whether, or how, Adorno responded to Mann's request.

2 On 29 May 1948 Thomas Mann had written to the publishing house J. C. B. Mohr in Tübingen:

> Dear Sirs, I am particularly gratified to learn that you are intending to publish Theodor Adorno's book 'The Philosophy of the New Music' and I should like to express my sincere hope that you will awaken fresh interest in this author, whose important work on Kierkegaard you have already published [in 1933], precisely through this no less significant publication.
>
> Dr Adorno is one of the finest, sharpest, and critically perceptive thinkers at work today. As a creative musician in his own right, he is also gifted with an analytical intelligence and an expressive facility of language which it is difficult to equal for conceptual precision and illuminating power. I cannot imagine anyone who is better placed than he to provide the public with such a perceptive and deeply grounded analysis of the situation in which music finds itself today. I am well acquainted with his work: he has been an ample source of encouragement and instruction for certain parts of 'Doctor Faustus', my novel based upon the life and work of a composer, and I should be particularly gratified if he could receive the recognition he properly deserves from the country in whose language his work is written.
>
> Above all I would wish that the French military authorities will do everything possible to facilitate your undertaking in this regard and will not hesitate to issue the required authorization and procure the necessary supplies of paper etc.
>
> Yours faithfully, Thomas Mann

(Cited from the *Tagebücher 1946–1948*, p. 924.) Excerpts from this letter were included in Mohr's publicity for Adorno's book and appeared on the jacket of *The Philosophy of the New Music* in the following year. The publisher's reply to Thomas Mann has apparently not survived.

T. W. ADORNO
316 So. Kenter Ave.
Los Angeles 24, Calif.

5 July 1948

My dear and highly esteemed Dr Mann,

I am delighted to pass on a few dates as requested.

I was born in Frankfurt in 1903. My father was a German Jew,[1] while my mother, herself a singer, was born to a French officer of Corsican, originally Genoese, origin and a German singer. I grew up in a family atmosphere shaped by highly theoretical (also political) and artistic, above all musical, interests.

I studied philosophy and music. Instead of deciding exclusively for one subject or the other, I have always had the feeling that my real vocation was to pursue one and the same thing in both of these different domains. In 1924 I received my doctorate with a dissertation on epistemology[2] and in 1931 I qualified as a university teacher in Frankfurt with my work on Kierkegaard.[3] I stayed in Frankfurt, where I taught philosophy until I was driven out by the Nazis in 1933.

I left Germany in 1934, initially continued my studies at the University of Oxford, and then followed the Institute of Social Research to New York.[4] I have lived in Los Angeles since 1941.

My relationship with the institute, and my friendship with Horkheimer, goes back to my early years as a student. This friendship cannot properly be separated from my dialectical perspective in general and my particular philosophical approach to society and history. The most important fruits of my collaboration with Horkheimer are the 'Dialectic of Enlightenment', which we published together,[5] and our memorial tribute to Walter Benjamin.[6]

In my musical studies I concentrated upon piano and composition, first with Bernhard Sekles[7] and Eduard Jung[8] in Frankfurt, and then with Alban Berg and Eduard Steuermann[9] in Vienna. My friendship with these musicians, as well as with Rudolf Kolisch[10] and Anton von Webern, has proved aesthetically decisive for me. In 1928–1931 I acted as editor of the Viennese journal 'Anbruch',[11] which strongly supported the cause of radical modern music.

This interaction between my musical and social-philosophical interests has already found expression, apart from some published excerpts from a work on Richard Wagner, in a number of studies in German and English,[12] the majority of which appeared in the 'Zeitschrift für

Sozialforschung'. The book on 'The Philosophy of the New Music', which is shortly to appear in Germany, effectively sums up, for the present, the results of these earlier studies. The first part of the book, already written in 1941, discusses Schönberg and his school, and the dodecaphonic technique. Although the book presents him unambiguously as the greatest living composer, it also argues that this objectively necessary constructive contribution to music also threatens, for equally objective reasons, and behind the composer's back as it were, to revert to something dark and mythological. The second part of the book, which I have only recently completed, discusses Stravinsky, rejects the possibility of a musical 'restoration' and reveals the inner connection between this idea and the regressive tendencies of the age. For more than ten years I have also been working on a book on Beethoven that addresses both philosophical and compositional issues.[13]

In addition to my writings on musical subjects I should also mention 'Minima Moralia', my recent collection of aphorisms.[14]

Perhaps it will not seem too immodest if I could ask you to lay greater emphasis upon my intellectual and imaginative contribution to Leverkühn's oeuvre and his aesthetic outlook than upon the provision of purely material information in this connection.

It is with the greatest excitement that I anticipate this ascent to immortality by the back door which your 'Story of a Novel' will vouchsafe me. I hardly need to say what it means to me that you have recognized some truth in my eccentric investigations and now intend to bring it into the full light of day. And I must already express my thanks to you for this here and now.

With the deepest respect,
Yours, [Teddie Adorno]

SOURCE: O: TS (carbon copy); Theodor W. Adorno Archive, Frankfurt am Main.

1 The Frankfurt businessman Oscar Wiesengrund (1870–1946) and his wife, the singer Maria Calvelli-Adorno (1864–1952), had left Germany in early 1939. They arrived in Cuba first but were able to settle in New York by the middle of 1940.

2 Adorno received his doctorate under the Frankfurt philosopher Hans Cornelius in 1924 with his dissertation 'Die Transzendenz des Dinglichen und Noematischen in Husserls Philosophie'. The work remained unpublished during Adorno's lifetime (see GS 1, pp. 7–77).

3 Adorno had written his post-doctoral dissertation *Kierkegaard: Construction of the Aesthetic* in 1929–30. It appeared in a heavily revised book form in Tübingen in 1933 (see GS 2, pp. 7–213).

4 The Institut für Sozialforschung, originally founded in Frankfurt in 1923, adopted this name when it was re-established in the United States. After the National Socialist seizure of power the institute was relocated initially in Geneva, and then in 1934 at Columbia University in New York.

5 See Letter 2, note 3, above.

6 Adorno is referring to the hectograph volume *Walter Benjamin zum Gedächtnis* [In Memory of Walter Benjamin], a 'special number' of the *Zeitschrift für Sozialforschung*, which officially ceased publication in 1941. Walter Benjamin's 'Theses on the Philosophy of History' appeared for the first time in this volume, which was published in Los Angeles under the auspices of the institute.

7 The composer Bernhard Sekles (1872–1934) was director of the Hoch'sche Conservatory in Frankfurt am Main from 1923 until the Nazi seizure of power in 1933. In a letter to his future teacher Alban Berg (1885–1935) Adorno wrote on 5 February 1925: 'My first compositional attempts were also made at an early age; I taught myself harmonic theory, and in 1919 came to Bernhard Sekles with songs and chamber music. I have been his student since; most recently, I have been working on five- and eight-part vocal counterpoint with him' (Theodor W. Adorno and Alban Berg, *Briefwechsel 1925–1935*, ed. Henri Lonitz, Frankfurt am Main, 1997, p. 9; English translation: *Correspondence 1925–1935*, trans. Wieland Hoban, Cambridge, 2005, p. 3 [translation amended].

8 In 1921 Adorno took private piano lessons with Eduard Jung (1884–1959), who also taught at the Hoch'sche Conservatory in Frankfurt.

9 The pianist and composer Eduard Steuermann (1892–1964), with whom Adorno studied piano in 1925 in Vienna, had lived in New York since 1937. See Adorno's personal tribute 'Nach Steuermanns Tod' (GS 17, pp. 311–17), and 'Die Komponisten Eduard Steuermann und Theodor W. Adorno: Aus ihrem Briefwechsel', in *Adorno-Noten*, ed. Rolf Tiedemann, Berlin, 1984, pp. 40–72.

10 Adorno had met the musician Rudolf Kolisch (1896–1978), violinist and leader of the Kolisch Quartet, and a pupil of Schoenberg, during his period of study in Vienna. In 1935 Adorno and Kolisch had planned to bring out a collaborative work on the theory of musical reproduction. For the sections which Adorno himself wrote between 1946 and 1959, see Theodor W. Adorno, *Nachgelassene Schriften*, Vol. 2: *Aufzeichnungen zu einer Theorie der musikalischen Reproduktion*, ed. Henri Lonitz, Frankfurt am Main, 2001. Kolisch was touring the USA with his quartet when war unexpectedly broke out in Europe in 1939 and he never actually returned to Germany. From 1944 he taught violin and chamber music at the University of Wisconsin.

11 The *Musikblätter des Anbruch*, published in Vienna under the auspices of Universal Edition, was known after 1929 simply as *Anbruch*. Although Paul Stefan (1879–1943) was the general editor from 1923 onwards, Adorno unofficially assumed editorial responsibility for the journal in 1929. See

Adorno's 'Exposé zur Neugestaltung der Zeitschrift "Zum Anbruch"' (*GS* 19, pp. 595–604) and the text which he published anonymously in the journal in 1929, 'Zum Jahrgang 1929 des "Anbruch"' (*GS* 19, pp. 605–8).

12 See Theodor W. Adorno: 'Über Jazz' [On Jazz] from 1936 (first published in the *Zeitschrift für Sozialforschung* 5, 1937; *GS* 17, pp. 74–100); 'Glosse über Sibelius' [Note on Sibelius] (*ZfS* 6, 1938; *GS* 17, pp. 247–52); 'Über den Fetischcharakter in der Musik und die Regression des Hörens' [On the Fetish Character in Music and the Regression of Listening] (*ZfS* 7, 1938; *GS* 14, pp. 14–50; English translation: *The Essential Frankfurt Reader*, ed. A. Arato and E. Gebhard, Oxford, 1978, pp. 270–99). See also Adorno's studies on the 'NBC Music Appreciation Hour' and the 'Radio Symphony', which he had intended to publish in a volume provisionally entitled 'Currents of Music: Elements of a Radio Theory' (Theodor W. Adorno, *Nachgelassene Schriften*, Vol. 3). Adorno's book *Philosophie der neuen Musik* was published by J. C. B. Mohr, Tübingen, in 1949 (*GS* 12; English translation: *The Philosophy of Modern Music*, trans. A. G. Mitchell and W. V. Blomster, New York, 1973).

13 Adorno never completed this work which he had been planning since 1934. The numerous notes and fragments that fill his notebooks in connection with this project, spanning a period of more than thirty years, have been published posthumously. (See Theodor W. Adorno, *Nachgelassene Schriften*, Vol. 1: *Beethoven: Philosophie der Musik: Fragmente und Texte*, ed. Rolf Tiedemann, Frankfurt am Main, 1993; English translation: *Beethoven: The Philosophy of Music*, trans. E. Jephcott, Cambridge, 1998.)

14 Adorno's collection of aphorisms, subtitled 'Reflections from Damaged Life', was published in Germany in 1951 (*GS* 4, pp. 7–281; English translation: *Minima Moralia*, trans. E. Jephcott, London, 1974).

12 THOMAS MANN TO THEODOR W. ADORNO
PACIFIC PALISADES, 12.7.1948

THOMAS MANN   1550
                              SAN REMO DRIVE
                    PACIFIC PALISADES, CALIFORNIA

                                       12 July 48

Dear Dr Adorno,

Heartfelt thanks for your expression of sympathy.[1] Klaus is physically restored, and for the moment is staying at Bruno Walter's along with Erika,[2] who is attending to his psychological well-being. I am rather angry with him for inflicting all this on his mother.[3] She is so understanding about everything – and I am too. This has spoilt him.

The situation remains dangerous. My two sisters committed

27

suicide,[4] and Klaus has much of the eldest sister about him. He has the same impulse within him, and this is only encouraged by current circumstances – except that he has a parental home he can always rely on, though he naturally does not wish to be dependent in this respect.

It is a good sign at least that he curses the 'publicity' surrounding the incident precisely because 'this makes it so hard to start over again'.

Your critique of Egk[5] betrays a sharp and serious wit. I found it tremendously amusing. I gave it to my brother-in-law[6] to read so he could appreciate just how rigorous, how respectful of tradition, this area of thought[7] can be – one which, like my dear friend Walter, he despises as anti-musical.

Until we meet again soon,

Yours,

Thomas Mann

SOURCE: O: MS with printed letterhead; Theodor W. Adorno Archive, Frankfurt am Main. Fp: *Briefe III*, p. 37.

1 The writer Klaus Mann (1906–1949), Thomas Mann's eldest son, had attempted to commit suicide on the night of 10 to 11 July 1948. No written record of Adorno's 'expression of sympathy' appears to have survived.

2 The actress and writer Erika Mann (1905–1969), Thomas Mann's eldest daughter.

3 Katia Mann, née Pringsheim (1883–1980), who had married Thomas Mann in 1905. From 1954 until her death she lived in Kilchberg on Lake Zurich. In 1974 Elisabeth Plessen and Michael Mann published her memoirs under the title *Katia Mann: Meine ungeschriebenen Memoiren*.

4 Thomas Mann's eldest sister Julia Löhr-Mann (1877–1927), the 'model' for the character of Ines Rodde in *Doctor Faustus*, and the actress Carla Mann (1881–1910), who also inspired the character of Clarissa in the novel.

5 Adorno's critical review of the Piano Sonata by Werner Egk (1901–1983), entitled 'Egkomion', remained unpublished during Adorno's lifetime (see *GS* 19, pp. 334–40). It is clear that it had already been written by 1948, and not in 1950, as the editors of Adorno's *Complete Writings* believed.

6 The composer, conductor and music teacher Klaus Pringsheim (1883–1972), Katia Mann's twin brother, and pupil of Gustav Mahler, was invited in 1933 to become the director of the Royal Japanese Academy of Music (he had been director of the Max Reinhard Bühne in Berlin until 1931). Pringsheim lost his position in Japan for political reasons in 1937 and eventually emigrated to California in 1946.

7 Mann is probably referring to the field of music theory.

THOMAS MANN
1550
SAN REMO DRIVE
PACIFIC PALISADES, CALIFORNIA

11. xii. 1948

Dear Dr Adorno,
You have to read this – firstly because Schönberg describes you as an 'informer',[1] and secondly because I am sure you can hardly be indifferent to his current state of mind.

The journal sent me this copy of what he has written. I am not sure whether they have yet received the English translation of my own reply. But if not, I do not think it really matters very much. I believe Schönberg's letter speaks for itself.

It would probably be best if you say nothing about the matter until my reply has appeared.

I am hoping to receive the proofs of the 'Story of a Novel' very shortly from Amsterdam, and will pass them on to you as soon as I do.

I would also be grateful if you could return the letter and the reply.

Greetings from one household to another,
Yours,
T. M.

SOURCE: O: MS with printed letterhead; Theodor W. Adorno Archive, Frankfurt am Main. Fp: *Briefe III*, p. 62.

1 Arnold Schoenberg (1874–1951) was particularly displeased with Thomas Mann for having presented Adrian Leverkühn as the inventor of the dodecaphonic method without even mentioning Schoenberg's name. In February 1948 Schoenberg sent Thomas Mann an article which he had composed for an imaginary 'Encyclopaedia Americana' for the year 1988. Writing under the pseudonym Hugo Triebsamen, he attempted to suggest the damage which he believed the character of Leverkühn could well inflict upon his own subsequent reputation. The article presents Thomas Mann as a writer who was originally a musician and the true inventor of the dodecaphonic technique. The writer suffers in silence when a certain thieving composer called Schoenberg appropriates this discovery for himself. It is only in *Doctor Faustus* that the writer openly proclaims this spiritual-musical property as his own. For Thomas Mann's initial attempt to reassure Schoenberg by letter on 17 February 1948, see *Briefe III*, p. 22f.

On 25 February 1948 Schoenberg attempted to explain himself to Mann in a rather conciliatory letter which also referred to the pseudonymous author of the article, the 'synthetic Hugo Triebsamen whom I produced by combining Hugo Riemann with Dr Rubsamen'. At Schoenberg's request Mann agreed to write a postscript for inclusion in subsequent editions of *Doctor Faustus* which would enlighten the reader about the true originator of the compositional technique described in chapter 22 of the novel. The postscript duly appeared in the Suhrkamp edition of 1948:

> Es scheint nicht überflüssig, den Leser zu verständigen, dass die im XXII. Kapitel dargestellte Kompositionsart, Zwölfton- oder Reihentechnik genannt, in Wahrheit das geistige Eigentum eines zeitgenössischen Komponisten und Theoretikers, Arnold Schoenbergs, ist und von mir in bestimmtem ideellem Zusammenhang auf eine frei erfundene Musikerpersönlichkeit, den tragischen Helden meines Romans, übertragen wurde. Überhaupt sind die musiktheoretischen Teile des Buches in manchen Einzelheiten der Schoenberg'schen *Harmonielehre* verpflichtet.

Thomas Mann

The postscript reads as follows in Helen Lowe-Porter's original English translation of the work:

> It does not seem supererogatory to inform the reader that the form of musical composition delineated in chapter XXII, known as the twelve-tone or row system, is in truth the intellectual property of a contemporary composer and theoretician, Arnold Schönberg. I have transferred this technique in a certain ideational context to the fictitious figure of a musician, the tragic hero of my novel. In fact, the passages of this book that deal with musical theory are indebted in numerous details to Schönberg's *Harmonielehre*.

Schoenberg initially appeared to be entirely satisfied by Thomas Mann's clarifications and wrote to this effect on 15 October 1948: 'I am very pleased that you have been kind enough to respect my wish to protect myself from the incompetence of all future historians of music [. . .] I was firmly convinced that I should expect no less from you than I do from myself, and I am very pleased that my trust has indeed been rewarded in this respect' (Thomas Mann, *Tagebücher 1946–1948*, p. 813). But it soon transpired that the controversy was far from over. On 13 November 1948 Schoenberg despatched an angry open letter, specifically aimed at Mann, to the *Saturday Review of Literature*. He complained that Mann's reference in the postscript to 'a contemporary composer and theoretician' only served to 'belittle' his own work and character: 'Yet in two or three decades we shall see who is the contemporary of whom.' Schoenberg felt that his discovery of the dodecaphonic technique had not properly been acknowledged, and had this to say about Mann's detailed discussion of 'the method of composing with twelve tones': 'The advisor and instructor [in the English version he had simply written 'informer'] was an earlier student of my deceased friend Alban Berg, namely Herr Wiesengrund-Adorno. He is thoroughly familiar with the actual details of this technique and was therefore quite capable of providing Herr Mann with a reasonably precise description of everything which one layman – the writer – requires in order to convince another layman – the reader – that he really understands what is at issue here.' The *Saturday Review of Literature* had sent Mann a copy of Schoenberg's letter in order to give him an opportunity to write a direct letter of reply, with the intention of publishing both letters together in English trans-lation (see 'Letters to the Editor: "Doctor Faustus" Schönberg?', *Saturday Review of Literature*, 32 (1 January 1949), pp. 22–3; the original German version of the letters appeared under the title 'Der Eigentliche' in the March issue of the journal *Monat*, 1/6, pp. 76–8). Mann's letter of reply to Schoenberg of 10 December 1948, in which he makes no mention of Adorno, concludes with the following words: 'Instead of smiling indulgently upon my book simply as an example of contemporary literature, and one which bears witness to his own powerful influence upon the musical culture of our epoch, Schoenberg interprets it as an expression of theft and insult. It is a painful drama to behold how an important man, in all too understandable over-irritation because of a life which has wavered between adoration and neglect, almost wilfully burrows into ideas of theft and persecution and loses himself in poisonous quarrels. May he rise above bitterness and distrust and find peace in the secure consciousness of his greatness and fame' (Thomas Mann, 'An die "Saturday Review of Literature"', repr. in *Reden und Aufsätze III, GW XI*, pp. 683–5). Although the 'correspondence' between Mann and Schoenberg effectively lapsed at this point, the composer resumed the polemic a year later, in the autumn of 1949 (see Letter 16 and the relevant note below).

14 THEODOR W. ADORNO TO THOMAS MANN
   SANTA MONICA, 19.7.1949

803 Yale Str.
Santa Monica, Calif.

19 July 1949

My dear and highly esteemed Dr Mann,
   Many thanks for the dedication copy of the 'Genesis',[1] which I received with the greatest of pleasure a couple of days ago. You can easily imagine how delighted I felt upon reading it – the even and unruffled serenity of the chapter on the operation[2] is a true masterpiece.
   I spent a most stimulating afternoon with Dr Pringsheim, who keeps me informed about you all the time. I am relieved to learn that somehow you have both been able to withstand the terrible blow that has befallen you.[3]
   Your imminent trip to Germany[4] will certainly prove a great psycho-logical trial, but on the other hand, given the extraordinary affective implications of everything connected with this return, it will probably also produce a certain liberating sense of release, not to mention the eminently moral significance which your visit to Germany will possess in any event. I wish you the very best imaginable in this regard.

31

The 'Philosophy of the New Music' is currently in press and should be out by the autumn. As far as 'Minima Moralia' is concerned, things are still hanging in the air on account of the terrible problems with the layout.[5] I have spent the whole of the summer in detailed revision of the very substantial volume on 'The Authoritarian Personality',[6] the great collective project of the institute, which will be published by Harpers in the autumn.

Heartfelt greetings from Gretel[7] and myself to you both, and to Erika

With the deepest respect,

Yours, [Teddie Adorno]

SOURCE: O: TS (carbon copy); Theodor W. Adorno Archive, Frankfurt am Main.

1 The copy in question has not survived in Adorno's personal library.

2 In chapter 12 Mann describes his stay in Billings Hospital in Chicago, where his lung operation was performed in 1946.

3 On 21 May 1949 Klaus Mann had died after taking an overdose of sleeping tablets.

4 Thomas Mann visited Germany between 23 July and 5 August. On 25 July he was awarded the Goethe Prize of the City of Frankfurt and delivered a speech in the Paulskirche entitled 'Ansprache im Goethejahr'. He repeated the speech on 1 August in Weimar, where he received another Goethe Prize, with a slightly modified introduction, under the title 'Ansprache in Weimar'. During the same trip Mann also visited Stuttgart, Munich, Nuremberg and Eisenach.

5 Adorno is presumably referring to the publisher's final decision to go ahead with the book and agree a specific date for publication. The relevant contract was finalized only on 25 September 1950 (see Letters 17 and 21 below).

6 See *The Authoritarian Personality*, by T. W. Adorno, Else Frenkel-Brunswik, Daniel J. Levinson and R. Nevitt Sanford, in collaboration with Betty Aron, Maria Hertz Levinson and William Morrow, New York, 1950 (Studies in Prejudice, Vol. 1). The volume, produced in California between 1944 and 1949, was a result of a collaboration between the Institute for Social Research and the Berkeley Public Opinion Study Group. It was centrally concerned with developing the 'Fascism Scale', the so-called F-scale, which continued to play an important role in the studies which the institute later carried out in Germany. Adorno described this broadly successful collaboration with the Berkeley Group in his essay 'Scientific Experiences in America' (see *GS* 10.2, pp. 721–30; English translation in *Critical Models: Interventions and Catchwords*, trans. H. Pickford, New York, 1998, pp. 215–42). For the chapters which Adorno prepared, either on his own or in collaboration with others, see *GS* 9.1, pp. 143–509.

7 Gretel Adorno (1902–1993), née Karplus, had married Adorno in 1937.

28 December 1949

Frankfurt a. M.
Liebigstrasse 19 III, bei Irmer

My dear and esteemed Dr Mann,

I know it is hardly sufficient to excuse my unduly long silence simply by mentioning the great flurry of work and experience that has overtaken me since my very first day in Paris.[1] But perhaps what I can best express here is the extraordinary difficulty of doing real justice to this experience, and indeed the great responsibility I feel in undertaking to describe for you the situation in Germany. As far as the aforementioned difficulty is concerned, it appears to be so rooted in the object itself that I am sure that even you will have encountered it too. For there is something peculiarly amorphous, intangible and shapeless about the experience. Extremely close observation of the Nuremberg trials[2] has revealed how this unspeakable guilt almost dissolves away into nothing, and the process appears to be repeated in even the most trivial aspects of everyday life. The most drastic expression of this is the fact that, apart from a couple of total and touchingly puppet-like villains, I still have not encountered any Nazis here – not simply in the ironic sense that people will not admit to having been Nazis, but in the far more disturbing sense that they believe they never were Nazis, that they have utterly and entirely repressed this. And, indeed, one could even speculate that they really 'were' not Nazis insofar as the fascist dictatorship, in view of its empty and humanly alienated character, was never appropriated like a bourgeois system of social life, but always remained at once alien and tolerated, a malign opportunity and a hope, something beyond identification – and this makes it demonically easy today to entertain a good conscience precisely where the bad one lives. 'We Germans', as an otherwise entirely decent student of mine[3] (currently researching the more esoteric aspects of Hegelian metaphysics) remarked in all innocence, 'have never taken anti-Semitism seriously.' He meant this quite sincerely, but I was forced to remind him of Auschwitz. It is highly instructive to consider people's relationship to these matters. I have observed that those who do identify in some respect with Hitlerism or the newly defined nationalism all steadfastly claim that they really knew nothing about the worst excesses throughout the whole period of the war – although those explicitly involved in the internal opposition can confirm what is clear to the simplest human intelligence: that everything was certainly known from 1943 onwards. It is so difficult to feel at ease in an environment where you

33

must constantly rely on your own intuitions, while the lie detector which is itself a part of the horror is what is really required. That these events elude all adequate experience also has the paradoxical result that one hardly realizes this fact. If I am honest, I must confess I always need a moment of reflection just to remind myself that my neighbour in the tram could actually have been an executioner.

My own situation is also partly responsible for this difficulty of feeling properly at ease here. For I have been plunged into the most intensive work with numbers of younger people,[4] and these same people – full-time students of philosophy for the most part – constitute what one is accustomed in current language to call an elite. Of course, immersed in the concrete commitments of work and surrounded by the temptations of vanity, one tends to interpret things in the best possible light, and, even if one can be very deluded in this respect, these students here make things very easy for me. All the same, after recently delivering a lecture on society and urban development[5] at the Technical College in Darmstadt, I certainly do not think one can really talk of any 'loss of standards' among the young in the academic context. And here I am thinking not so much of the student participation in the collegium, but in the seminar which has been focusing on Kant's transcendental dialectic as a somewhat unconventional preparation for the study of Hegel. I can hardly begin to describe the passionate engagement of the students, which clearly has more to do with the material itself than with me, and they are so enthusiastic that I actually have considerable difficulty making my own voice heard. This extends from relatively external things – it is often hardly possible to bring the seminar to a close at the appointed time and the youngsters have even asked me to continue the seminar throughout the vacation – to the actual content of the discussions themselves. We are discussing extremely obscure questions at the very limits of logic and metaphysics, but precisely as if they were political issues – perhaps because there is in truth no longer any politics. I am tempted to compare it with a talmudic school. It sometimes seems to me as though the spirits of the murdered Jews have entered into our German intellectuals. It is particularly characteristic that we are almost always concerned with questions of interpretation, and hardly ever with questions of the actual truth of a theory – a play of spirit with itself that would have earned any of us the reproach of contemptible aestheticism if we had done the same. It is as if spirit, denied the possibility of realizing itself externally and thereby cut off from its proper theoretical object, now circles within itself and simply rests content with sharpening its own weapons.

A kind of war game after all, you may ask, thus indicating the problem which cannot ultimately be avoided: are the Germans still Nazis, or have they once again become Nazis? I do not think so, and hope that I am not deceiving myself on this decisive point. It is not exactly as though they have changed their attitudes, or have really undergone the famous transformation that was never credible even in its Sternbergerian form.[6] One cannot grasp this process in psychological terms, but only from the political perspective. And the decisive consideration I believe is this: Germany has ceased to be a political subject at all, and politics is now simply role play – and everyone knows as much since people are not stupid. They sense they are now part of the greater conflict of the two great constellations of power, and they literally seek to profit from the fact, but the idea that there is any serious prospect of affecting historical events from within Germany – this is something I have never encountered here in either thought or gesture. As far as the outside world is concerned they would rather cling to the prevailing powers in order to survive – as 'poor in deeds and rich in thoughts',[7] as if we were still in the year 1800. Not that there is any lack of reactionary sentiments in the air. The celebrated quest for genuine foundations, for some external source of authority rather than one derived from rigorous reflection, already harbours a reactionary dimension, and the intellectuals like to call this 'ontology', whether it be Heideggerian or Catholic in inspiration. But these reactionary tendencies are without question more positive-Christian than traditionally fascist in character. If there is one place for us today where critical reflection should concentrate its efforts it is precisely this one. And it is in this context that we should mention the very peculiar role played by Herr Jünger,[8] a wretchedly meretricious writer who has mutated from his appalling quondam steeliness into an, if possible, even more appalling second-hand George complete with gleaming fronds, iridescent scales, and a mass of false concretion, and upon whom those representatives of 'youth' who are pleased to describe themselves as such would now appear to dote. Fortunately he has so little talent that his current success already implies its own negation. It is the kind of short-lived immortality enjoyed by Tieck after 1832.[9]

Nonetheless, these things must prove irksome in the context of your own indescribable 'engagement' with the Germans, and you will be distressed by the idiotic attacks which the vulgar Catholics in particular[10] tend to direct against you – perhaps more distressed than if you were actually over here, where you might easily recognize in such polemics some kind of obscure impulse to incite an argument. Perhaps you will permit me to express a few thoughts of my own concerning the Germans and their relationship to you. From the psychoanalytic point of view this relationship is emotionally saturated to an incredible degree – with all the ambivalence which the concept of saturation implies, with much that is twisted, wrecked and unrepentant, but also with the love that lies behind the mechanisms of repression. It is as if they cannot be rid of you, and, since they do not dare to love, they are driven to insult you (naturally there are also many other things in play, but then you already realize that – I am speaking here only of the remarkable resistance you encounter here). And why is it that they do not dare to love? Once again, this is difficult to explain other than in psychological terms, although in the final analysis it is reactive social forms themselves which are responsible. You are the one – and the only one, it seems to me, given the vainly impotent character of the confessions that have already been expressed by Jaspers and Niemöller[11] – who has really brought something of the Germans' repressed guilt to the surface of consciousness, who has actually 'addressed' them in the theological sense which this word once possessed. And repudiation is precisely their response to this, an attempt to repress once again what was inadequately repressed before. In other words, we are dealing here with an authentic case of projection. The Marktredwitz nonsense[12] of people of all social ranks, states and zones is precisely a way of transferring onto you everything with which you have burdened the indignant citizens whom you understand only too well. I hardly need to say that I do not thereby mean to trivialize the wretched common front of moralism and philistinism, of people like Holthusen[13] and Schlabrendorf[14] – but merely, perhaps, by recognizing the nature of the remarkable opposition which you have provoked, to remove something of the sting which might otherwise cause you occasional discomfort.

On account of the relationship between your Faustus novel and my philosophy of music, which only feeds the need for such projections, I have developed an acute sense for this sort of thing, and cannot really deny how much I am flattered by such attacks. In this connection it might amuse you to know that a quarter of all copies of my 'Philosophy of the New Music' have already been sold in an extremely short period of time – doubtless to the considerable disappointment of readers who must have been expecting a pleasant day out to the theatre. You will also be aware that certain Christian critics, such as Doflein[15] and Horst,[16] have officially identified me as your very own devil – and hopefully you will feel as much at home in this infernal climate as I do myself. For the rest, I am exceptionally well physically, three times as fresh and prepared for work as I felt in western climes, and spared the old headaches – a strangely promising start for a professionally homeless individual in his own homeland. – Hans Mayer has paid me a visit,[17] and we had a most agreeable conversation which would have set your ears tingling. The German edition of the book on film music[18] has turned out less agreeably, with a dreadful preface by the supposed co-author, whose name alone officially appears on the book, and a host of unauthorized changes in the text. – I was very impressed by Mayer's volume of essays 'Literature in an Age of Transition',[19] and I have learned a good deal from the 'Works and Forms' of my old teacher Karl Reinhardt,[20] a late bloom from the tradition of George at its best and one in which you might also find much of interest. – Has Leibowitz sent you a copy of his extremely competent, if unreservedly apologetic, 'Introduction à la musique de douze sons'?[21] If not, I can get him to do so.

May you all begin the new year most happily and in the very best of health! You know of course what my egoism most of all desires, and I should be infinitely grateful with regard to this matter – namely 'Krull' – if you could say a word or two about how your work is progressing.

I was particularly put in mind of you when I visited the Goethe Museum and my eye fell upon the manuscript of his poem 'To the Rising Full Moon'.[22] I found myself wondering whether, amid the historical debris, you have also gazed upon these indescribable Dornburg strophes with a similar sense of astonishment? Whether my gaze has followed yours?

With the most heartfelt respect,

Yours faithfully,

Teddie Adorno

SOURCE: O: TS with handwritten corrections by the author; Thomas Mann Archive, Zurich. Pp: *Tagebücher 1949–1950*, p. 506f.

1 Adorno returned to Europe on the *Queen Elizabeth* at the end of October 1949. He probably arrived in Paris on 27 October, where he stayed at the Hotel Lutetia. He travelled on to Frankfurt on 2 November.

2 In the course of the Nuremberg trials, between October 1945 and 30 September 1946, the International Court, authorized by the treaty signed by the four occupying powers on 8 August 1945, sentenced twenty-four major war criminals, condemning twelve of them to death. The National Socialist Führer Corps, the Gestapo, the SD and the SS were all declared criminal organizations. Further trials of lawyers, SS doctors, concentration camp commandants, diplomats, generals, industrialists and high-level officials and civil servants active under the former regime soon followed.

3 It has not been possible to identify the individual in question.

4 In the winter semester of 1949–50 Adorno resumed his former academic activities in Frankfurt. He initially deputized for Max Horkheimer, but from the summer semester of 1950 he took up the position of *Privatdozent* which he had been forced to abandon in 1933.

5 Adorno had spoken on this subject at the colloquium of the Technical College in Darmstadt on 9 December 1949. The lecture was delivered in the context of the 'Darmstädter Gemeindestudie' sanctioned by the American

military administration in 1949–52 with the direct participation of the Institute for Social Research. These studies resulted in nine monographs, for which Adorno co-authored the introductions with Max Rolfes, published in eight volumes between 1952 and 1954 (see GS 20.2, pp. 605–39).

6 The journalist and writer Dolf Sternberger (1907–1989) had been editor of the *Frankfurter Zeitung* between 1933 and 1943. He also edited the monthly journal *Die Wandlung* [The Transformation] in Heidelberg between 1945 and 1949. Other editors of the same journal included Karl Jaspers, Alfred Weber (1868–1958) and Marie Luise Kaschnitz (1901–1974). From 1955 Sternberger taught political science at the University of Heidelberg.

7 The last line of the first strophe of Friedrich Hölderlin's poem 'An die Deutschen' [To the Germans]: 'Spottet ja nicht des Kinds, wenn es mit Peitsch und Sporn / Auf dem Rosse von Holz mutig und gross sich dünkt, / Denn, ihr Deutschen, auch ihr seid / Tatenarm und gedankenvoll' [Never scorn the child who sits with whip and spur / Astride his wooden horse and deems himself brave and great, / You Germans, for you too are/Poor in deeds and rich in thoughts.]

8 The writer Ernst Jünger (1895–1998), herald of 'heroic nihilism' and singer of 'material slaughter and the total worker's state'. After the Hitler regime had realized many of his demands Jünger adopted a rather cooler and more distanced view of the National Socialist state. His most popular writings included *In Stahlgewittern* [In Storms of Steel] of 1920 and *Auf den Marmorklippen* [On Marble Cliffs] of 1939. Opponents of the regime mistakenly interpreted the latter work as a coded critique of the National Socialist system, and some attempted to claim Jünger as a member of the conservative opposition which assumed a policy of so-called inner emigration. His war diaries appeared in Tübingen in 1949 under the title *Strahlungen* [Light Shafts] and his utopian novel *Heliopolis* was published in the same year. Adorno may here be alluding to *Heliopolis*, which reveals a turn towards a somewhat theologically coloured humanism.

9 It is possible that Adorno was thinking of Tieck's popularity after about 1832 (the year of Goethe's death) before his work effectively fell into oblivion in the 1840s. Tieck, whom many had initially regarded as a possible successor to Goethe, died in 1853.

10 It is not possible to identify the particular individuals Adorno was alluding to here.

11 See Karl Jaspers, *Die Schuldfrage* [The Question of Guilt] (Heidelberg, 1946). Karl Jaspers (1883–1969) had been banned from teaching in Germany between 1937 and 1945 and had recently accepted a chair at the University of Basel in 1948. He used the relevant essay to introduce his 'Lectures on the Spiritual Situation of Germany, Delivered [in Heidelberg] in the Winter Semester of 1945–1946' (according to the preface of the published version). The Lutheran theologian Martin Niemöller (1892–1985) was arrested in 1937 and interned as a political prisoner in the concentration camps of Sachsenhausen and Dachau. He was regarded as the principal author of the

'Stuttgart Declaration of Guilt' which the Council of the Evangelical Church submitted to representatives of the ecumenical movement in October 1945. (See Martin Niemöller, *Reden 1945–1954*, Darmstadt, 1958, p. 322.)

12 After the writer's visit to Weimar in the German Democratic Republic the street named after Thomas Mann in Marktredwitz was officially renamed after Goethe instead.

13 Hans Egon Holthusen (1913–1997), a writer, literary critic, essayist and poet, pursued a career as an independent author in Munich. Mann is heavily criticized in Holthusen's book *Die Welt ohne Transzendenz: Eine Studie zu Thomas Manns Doktor Faustus und seinen Nebenschriften* [World without Transcendence: A Study of Thomas Mann's Dr Faustus and his other Writings].

14 The lawyer Fabian von Schlabrendorff (1907–1980) had already been a conservative opponent of National Socialism before 1933. He sympathized with the oppositional circle in the military that was centred around General Han Oster (1888–1945) and played a significant role in the two failed bomb attempts on Hitler's life in March 1943. He practised as a lawyer after 1945 and acted as a judge in the Federal Constitutional Court from 1967 to 1975. Among other things Schlabrendorff published a memoir entitled *Offiziere gegen Hitler* [Officers Against Hitler] in 1946. He repudiated the concept of collective guilt that tended to identify the German people as a whole with the National Socialist regime.

15 The musical writer and pedagogue Erich Doflein (1900–1977) taught at the Musikhochschule in Freiburg from 1947 onwards. In 1948 he became one of the founders of the Institute for New Music and Musical Education in Darmstadt. In the second part of a piece on Adorno's *Philosophy of the New Music* he also explicitly referred to *Doctor Faustus*: 'The divinatory power which the ailing Leverkühn derives from his secularized pact with the Devil and the lucid force of Adorno's deliberately paradoxical dialectic are the two extremes which here join hands: Adorno is the authentic Lucifer of this "Faustus". Yet his dialectic is condemned to paralysis. This combination of symbol and diagnosis drives the author to take refuge in the idea of fate. A tragic hero of cultural crisis is thereby dressed up as Faust.' (See Erich Doflein, 'Leverkühns Inspirator: Eine Philosophie der Neuen Musik', *Die Gegenwart* 4/22 (1949), pp. 22–4.)

16 The essayist, story writer and literary critic Karl August Horst (1913–1973) had described the collaboration between Adorno and Thomas Mann as a 'devil's pact' in which Mann himself had fallen victim to the 'devil of dialectic' (see 'Montierte Genialität', *Rheinischer Merkur*, 10 December 1949).

17 The lawyer, literary historian and essayist Hans Mayer (1907–2001), who had formerly lived as an exile in France and Switzerland, was invited in 1945 to take up an editorial position with Frankfurt Radio, where he also worked with Golo Mann. In 1948 he became professor of literary history at the University of Leipzig, although he left the German Democratic Republic and returned to the Federal Republic in 1963.

18 See Hanns Eisler, *Komposition für den Film* (Berlin, 1949). Adorno and Eisler had originally collaborated on the book in 1944, although Adorno himself contributed by far the greater part to the project (*GS 15*, Editorial Postscript, p. 405f.). It was published first of all in English, solely under Eisler's name (in New York in 1947), because Adorno was wary of becoming involved in the controversy in the United States surrounding the political opinions of Eisler's brother Gerhardt. Hanns Eisler himself was subsequently attacked as a communist sympathizer. In place of the original co-authored preface, Eisler supplied the first German edition with a 'vehemently anti-American preface and also adapted numerous details, through various additions and retouchings, to the official Soviet outlook. He even toned down certain passages on purely musical questions, such as the critique of Prokofiev's score for the film of Alexander Nevsky. But, above all, he popularized the language of the book to the detriment of its originally rigorous and pregnant expression. This disturbed the character of the entire book' (see Theodor W. Adorno, 'Remarks on the First Publication of the Original Text', *GS 15*, p. 144f.). The original text, in an edition prepared by Adorno, eventually appeared in Munich in 1969 (see *GS 15*, pp. 7–143; Theodor W. Adorno and Hanns Eisler, *Composing for the Films*, ed. Graham McCann, London, 1994).

19 See Hans Mayer, *Literatur der Übergangszeit: Essays* (Berlin, 1949). In addition to the specific pieces entitled 'Thomas Mann als bürgerlicher Schriftsteller' (pp. 156–63) and 'Thomas Manns Roman "Doktor Faustus" ' (pp. 164–76), the essay 'Kulturkrise und moderne Musik' (pp. 200–17) also makes reference to Adorno and Thomas Mann.

20 The classical philologist Karl Reinhardt (1886–1958) had held professorships in Marburg and Hamburg before moving to Frankfurt in 1923. His book *Von Werken und Formen: Vorträge und Aufsätze* was published in Godesberg in 1948. A copy of the book, with a handwritten dedication from the author dated May 1955, is preserved in the Thomas Mann Library in Zurich.

21 René Leibowitz (1913–1972) was a French composer and writer of Polish origin. Through his activities as both a writer and a conductor he consistently championed the works of Schoenberg and his students – he had himself pursued studies in harmony with Anton Webern in 1931–2 – and exercised a considerable influence upon the reception of their music in France. In 1945 he became director of Radiodiffusion Française. His book *Introduction à la musique de douze sons* was published in Paris in 1949.

22 See the three strophes of the poem which is dated 'Dornburg, 25.8.1828': 'Willst du mich sogleich verlassen? / Warst im Augenblick so nah! / Dich umfinstern Wolkenmassen, / Und nun bist du gar nicht da. // Doch du fühlst, wie ich betrübt bin, / Blickt dein Rand herauf als Stern! / Zeugest mir, dass ich geliebt bin, / Sei das Liebchen noch so fern. // So hinan denn! Hell und heller, / Reiner Bahn, in voller Pracht! / Schlägt mein Herz auch schmerzlich schneller, / Überselig ist die Nacht.' [Must you leave me, must I lose you? / For a moment you were near, / Now thick darkling clouds enfold you, / Now you fade and disappear. // But your gleaming rim consoles me, / Beacons like a rising star, /

Brings the words my darling tells me: / I am loved, though she is far. // Shine on then in brightest ardour, / Soar in pure triumphant flight! / Though my lonely heart beats harder, / Still this splendour fills the night.] (*Johann Wolfgang von Goethe. Selected Poetry*, trans. David Luke, London, 1999).

16 THOMAS MANN TO THEODOR W. ADORNO
PACIFIC PALISADES, 9.1.1950

THOMAS MANN

1550
SAN REMO DRIVE
PACIFIC PALISADES, CALIFORNIA

9 Jan. 1950

Dear Dr Adorno,

Very many thanks for your rich and interesting letter. It has been read repeatedly, and read aloud, and yesterday I had the opportunity to tell your dear wife[1] all about it when she came to lunch. At last we got round to meeting again! – it took so long to arrange only because I have been rather ill lately and have therefore felt quite unfit for social intercourse: I had contracted an infectious inflammation and swelling of the inner ear which left me virtually deaf for a while – a depressing condition further exacerbated by itching sensations throughout the night. Time-consuming medical treatment had brought some real improvement in this respect when I suddenly developed a serious inflammation of the throat which is still causing discomfort – probably the original infection which merely fled elsewhere after the initial medical exorcisms. I don't really know how to explain it, but the air itself seems haunted here, and I am really struck by just how fresh and well you feel over there in a homeland that has become foreign. And here in a foreign land that has become home we cannot help feeling we are in the wrong place, something which robs our own existence of a certain moral authority. But then again we have good reason to enjoy life here. I do love this house, which is quite perfect for me, and also love the country and the people, who have been very friendly and well disposed to us, even if the political atmosphere is becoming more and more unbreathable.[2] Only recently the Beverly Wilshire Hotel refused the use of its hall for a dinner of the Arts, Sciences and Professions Council[3] because a communist like Dr Mann[4] had been invited to speak. Of course this caused such an uproar in the community, and provoked such a flurry of telegrams to the hotel, that they eventually capitulated and offered us the hall after all. When my throat condition is better I shall turn up there and deliver the kind of serene speech that befits someone of my years. I actually have a good citizen's right to protest at such treatment since this year alone I have had to feed the jaws of the Cold War to the tune of 16,000 dollars in taxes. Was it for this that I laboured on Dr Faustus? I think not.

Would you believe that Schoenberg has fired off *another* broadside against you, me and the book? It appeared in a London journal called 'Musical Survey', though the article was so silly that the editor has described it rather apologetically as a 'character document'.[5] Among other things the author claims that no good has ever come to those who have offended him – of two women who did so, he says, one broke her leg and the other fell victim to some other unspecified affliction.[6] The whole thing is really beyond belief. I have written to him again[7] to say that, even if he still wants to run around as my enemy, he will never make me his.

At present I am still smiling benevolently upon the 'Confidence Man' from some distance since 'The Holy Sinner' is not yet finished, although I have made good progress with it. I can say that *nothing* now impedes my work schedule during the mornings. The 'penitent' is now on his savage stone,[8] and to describe his source of nourishment I have, or rather the monk has, borrowed the idea from Epicurus (and Lucretius)[9] of the 'uteri' of the earth and the 'milk' which she produced to feed the very first human beings. It is just such a 'tube', reaching right down into the earth, that has been left for Gregorius. One has to resort to such shifts. Hartmann *seems* to suggest something of the kind himself.[10]

Greetings to you all – and we wish the best for your continued happy musings with the children there,

Yours,

Thomas Mann

SOURCE: O: MS with printed letterhead; Theodor W. Adorno Archive, Frankfurt am Main. Fp: *Briefe III*, p. 127ff.

1 Gretel Adorno did not return to Germany until April 1950.

2 The words 'more and more unbreathable' are given in English in the text of Mann's letter.

3 Thomas Mann delivered a speech of thanks before the Southern California chapter of the Council of the Arts, Sciences and Professions on 14 January 1950 on receiving an award from the council (see *Tagebücher 1949–1950*, pp. 684–6). The official text of the latter reads as follows: 'Southern California Chapter, National Council of the Arts, Sciences and Professions award to Dr Thomas Mann for his distinguished contributions as author and citizen to the advancement of peace, intellectual freedom and a democratic culture. Los Angeles, California, January Fourteenth, 1950.

For the executive board signed Howard Koch, Chairman' (cited from *Briefe III*, p. 520f.).

4 Mann is alluding to the persecution of socialist and communist sympathizers which was just beginning to make itself felt in the United States. This development culminated a few years later in the hearings of the House Committee on Un-American Activities, under the chairmanship of the Wisconsin Senator Joseph R. McCarthy (1909–1957), a body that had originally been established in 1938 to investigate groups and individuals hostile to the American government. The FBI had also kept files on Mann since the 1930s.

5 See 'Further to the Schoenberg–Mann Controversy: By Arnold Schoenberg', *Music Survey*, 2/2 (1949), pp. 77–80. In his prefatory remarks Hans Keller says: 'In his letter accompanying the following communication, which we here publish for the first time, Schoenberg writes that the matter "may perhaps be be stale" by now. So it may, but the character document of a master never is. The authorized translation and the annotations are mine. H. K.'

6 Schoenberg had actually written: 'It is very peculiar that when someone hits at me in a particularly nasty way, fate seizes him by the collar.' There is no specific reference in the article to a woman breaking her leg.

7 See Thomas Mann's letter to Schoenberg of 19 December 1949, in which he says: 'Perhaps I can take this opportunity to ask a question: if I am to be subjected to a hailstorm of ever more grievous attacks, may I be permitted, in this extremity of need, to publish the letter which you sent me on 15 October 1948 after receiving a copy of the English edition of "Dr Faustus" containing the postscript, and in which you sincerely thank me for having fulfilled your own express wishes? [. . .] You are really attacking a bugbear of your imagination that is certainly not me. So I harbour no desire for revenge here. If you really wish to be my enemy – you will not succeed in making me into yours' (*Briefe III*, p. 122). Schoenberg finally replied to Mann in a conciliatory letter of 2–4 January 1950, which closes with the following words: 'If the hand that I believe is held out to me here is the hand of peace, if it truly signifies an offer of peace, I shall be the last not to grasp it at once and shake it in token of confirmation. In fact I have often thought of writing to you and saying: Let us bury the hatchet and show that on a certain level there is indeed always a chance of peace [. . .] One or the other of us will one day celebrate our "eightieth" – we shall not have to wait so very long – and this shall be a good occasion to put everything petty behind us, and do so for good' (cited from *Tagebücher 1949–1950*, p. 511f.). There would be no such public reconciliation, however, since Schoenberg died on 13 July 1951.

8 See the chapter entitled 'The Penance' in Thomas Mann's novel *Der Erwählte* (*GW* VII, pp. 189–95; English translation: *The Holy Sinner*, trans. H. Lowe-Porter, London, 1952, repr. 1997, pp. 167–72).

9 Thomas Mann had come upon this idea of anthropogenesis, as described by Lucretius and originally ascribed to Democritus by Epicurus, in an essay by Karl Kerényi (1897–1973). In July 1946 the author himself had sent Mann an offprint of his essay 'Urmensch und Mysterium' (*Eranos-Jahrbuch 1947*,

XV, Zurich, 1948, pp. 41–74). Mann wrote to Kerényi on 4 January 1950, a few days before his letter to Adorno: 'I am now busy re-reading your essay "Urmensch und Mysterium", surely one of the most remarkable things you have written. It is directly relevant to my work on "Gregorius", and especially to the question of how he manages to feed himself in the mountains. Hartmann von Aue already described this in a way that *slightly* recalls Epicurus's notion of the "uteri" of the earth and the nourishing milk which she originally offered to the very first human beings. By drawing on your own citations concerning the "tubes of skin" [*Schläuche*] I will develop this idea both more precisely and more fantastically than Hartmann does – he would surely be astonished to read my own version of the story' (*Briefe III*, p. 126). In the offprint Mann specifically marked the following excerpt from Book V of Lucretius's *De rerum natura* (lines 805ff.), which Kerényi cited in the German translation by Hermann Diels: 'Then it was that the earth brought forth the first mammals. There was a great superfluity of heat and moisture in the soil. So, wherever a suitable spot occurred, there grew up skins [*Schläuche*], clinging to the earth by roots. [Here Kerényi observed that the Diels translation 'relies on the ambiguity of the Latin word *uterus* which in the present context principally signifies *womb*.'] These, when the time was ripe, were burst open by the maturation of the embryos, rejecting moisture now and struggling for air. Then nature directed towards that spot the pores of the earth, making it open its veins and exude a juice resembling milk, just as nowadays every female when she has given birth is filled with sweet milk because all the flow of nourishment within her is directed into the breasts' (Karl Kerényi, loc. cit. p. 44f.; English translation adapted from Lucretius, *On the Nature of the Universe*, trans. R. E. Latham, Harmondsworth, 1951).

10 In California Thomas Mann managed to obtain an edition of the original Middle High German text of Hartmann von Aue's 'Gregorius' (*Die Werke Hartmanns von Aue*, Vol. IV: *Gregorius*, ed. Hermann Paul, Halle, 1882, in the *Altdeutschen Textbibliothek*, No. 2, 1948), but he was unable to find a modern German translation of the work. After making relevant enquiries with Professor Samuel Singer (1860–1948) in Bern, he eventually received a modern prose translation which Marga Bauer-Noeggerath, a colleague of Singer's, had prepared specifically for his use.

17   THEODOR W. ADORNO TO THOMAS MANN
     FRANKFURT AM MAIN, 3.6.1950

Frankfurt/Main, Liebigstr. 19[III]
3 June 1950

My dear and esteemed Dr Mann,
    I had continued to hope, in a corner of my heart, that you would decide to visit Germany after all and thus vouchsafe me the opportunity of greeting you here in Frankfurt. But since this is clearly not to

be, and my academic and institutional duties prevent me from leaving here at present, I should like to confess, at least in letter form, the deep significance which this symbolic day[1] possesses for me and to assure you that all my own good thoughts are with you at this time. And the most important one – apart from my hopes for your health – is that you may suffer as little as possible from the German trauma and transform it instead into what I call 'unsouled misery', into an objectified opposite from which the thorn of bodily experience has been extracted. For the unattractive reification of political life here surely demands as much. I should then further express that obstinate wish, once you have completed your legendary work,[2] with which I have burdened you so long already, that you will finish the book on Krull as the myth of the nineteenth century, one which may help at last to expiate the myth of the twentieth.

In this connection I was recently struck by a remark by Nietzsche[3] in the first volume of *Human, All Too Human*. It is not only a fine motto for Krull but also reads like an ancient Chinese saying which is not so inappropriate for expressing the relationship between recent modernity and the archaic past: 'The wittiest writers provoke a barely perceptible smile'. That is precisely what your Krull fragment does. And while this effect arises from an infinite sublimating of artistic means, from a kind of purification of everything that is usually called humour, this very un-European sublimation creates a distance which allows the world of our parents to petrify silently in such images as if it were already something paleontological. Recently I came across a church in Wilhelminian Wiesbaden which resembled a kind of protective guardian – will the Chief of Police who was promised in your Krull fragment[4] not also appear in the end as a sort of fossil? For I only ask, with a truly impassioned interest, that in this utterly decisive sphere – that of liberation from the fetters of bourgeois phantasmagoria – the work of art should redeem something of what philosophy has hitherto vainly struggled to grasp. From this you will appreciate how egotistical my wish really is, but I trust I may nonetheless expect forgiveness here from the truly humane heart of an artist who understands so well the nature of inhumanity.

I should be all too happy to report to you in person about the progress of my own German experience. In some ways Gretel has allowed the moment of negativity to exercise an increasing affect upon her. I am not thinking particularly of nationalism, neo-fascism or anti-Semitism in this respect, although the fact that I myself have seen very little of these things has certainly not led me to doubt that they still exist. But what strikes me as even more significant here is the phenomenon of German regression. The inarticulate character of political conviction, the readiness to submit to every manifestation of actual

45

power, the instant accommodation to whatever new situation emerges, all this is merely an aspect of the same regression. If it is true that the manipulative control of the masses always brings about a regressive formation of humanity, and if Hitler's drive for power essentially involved the realization of this development 'at a single stroke', we can only say that he, and the collapse that followed, has indeed succeeded in producing the required infantilization. And the products of culture, which are now literally consumed as if they were unattainable consumer goods, have already almost come to assume the function of playthings. One must acknowledge that the collective energy of the Germans was marshalled by the fascist enterprise to a hitherto unparalleled degree, and this itself has encouraged an attitude of 'everything or nothing'. And what is left resembles, from a metaphysical perspective, nothing so much as the actual ruins that already surround us physically: people who are damaged with respect to the ego, to autonomy, to spontaneity, who often almost appear to be fulfilling Spengler's wretched prophecies concerning the rise of the new cave dwellers.[5] Even now I have no wish to deny the real ferment at work here, but I do often wonder whether this is indeed a manifestation of our proverbial 'new life' or simply the swarm that comes crawling out once the stone has been lifted. It is often difficult, in these enervating circumstances, to banish a certain feeling of futility when attempting to begin work on anything new; and the former Californian location, which I sometimes resented because of its unreality, now seems to enjoy rather more reality than that which we can observe over here. In other words, one no longer feels at home anywhere; but then, of course, someone whose business is ultimately demythologization should hardly complain too much about this.

As far as my own work is concerned I would simply like to mention here that Suhrkamp[6] is still hoping to publish my book of aphorisms. He had even succeeded in winning over Bermann for the project, along with Podszus,[7] before serious disagreements arose – there is no question in my mind that I should now commit the project to him. In the meantime a longer work of mine on Husserl[8] has appeared in the *Archiv für Philosophie*, though not without provoking some scandal in certain quarters – which is only to be expected if one tries to let logic truly speak. You may already be aware that Rychner, in a rather sympathetic essay in *Die Tat*, has attempted to interpret my highly ambivalent radio lecture on 'The Resurrection of Culture'[9] as the conversion document of a former émigré – this is a most curious business. I have not been able to contemplate anything more substantial at present because Horkheimer and I are still both immersed in the work of re-establishing the institute,[10] in which HICOG and UNESCO have also expressed an extremely active interest. Have you cast a glance at

'The Authoritarian Personality', or perhaps condemned my philistine labours on such a volume? It is no sacred text, to be sure, but you may still find something in there which you would not entirely wish to repudiate.

I am afraid I must regard Lukács's big book on Hegel,[11] which I have worked through from beginning to end, as among my most depressing recent experiences. One can hardly credit such reification of consciousness in the very man who coined this concept in the first place.[12] Heidegger's essay in 'Holzwege' on the *Phenomenology of Spirit* is almost dialectical by comparison.[13] You may count yourself fortunate to be spared this kind of thing.

Enjoy your holidays, remember me if you should ever get to drink a mythical 'Berncasteler Doctor',[14] and allow yourself to be tempted, under one pretext or another, into visiting us here sometime.

Heartfelt greetings to both of you, and from Gretel too,

Yours,

Teddie Adorno

SOURCE: O: TS with handwritten corrections; Thomas Mann Archive, Zurich.

1 Thomas Mann's seventy-fifth birthday on 6 June 1950.

2 Adorno is referring to Mann's novel *Der Erwählte* [The Chosen One], which was completed on 26 October 1950. It appeared in English translation in 1952 under the title *The Holy Sinner*.

3 See Friedrich Nietzsche, *Human, All Too Human*, Part IV: 'From the Soul of Artists and Writers', Aphorism 186: 'Wit – The wittiest authors provoke a barely perceptible smile.'

4 Adorno is referring to the original version of Mann's novel which was published in Amsterdam in 1937. This edition contained the 'First Book', the so-called Book of Childhood, and five chapters from a 'Second Book' which is explicitly presented as 'fragmentary'. The passage to which Adorno alludes occurs in chapter 1 of the 'Second Book', where the narrator considers whether he should continue to recount his life story after such a long interruption: '[. . .] and as certain striking moments of my career appeared vividly before me, I was quite unable to believe that incidents which exercise so enlivening an effect upon me could fail to entertain the reading public as well. If I recall, for example, one of the great houses of Germany where, masquerading as a Belgian aristocrat, I sat in the midst of a distinguished company, chatting over coffee and cigars with the director of police, an unusually humane man with a deep understanding of the human heart, discussing the characteristics of confidence men and their appropriate punishment [. . .]' (Thomas Mann, *Bekenntnisse des Hochstaplers Felix Krull*, in *GW* VII, p. 323; English translation: *Confessions of Felix Krull, Confidence Man*,

trans. D. Lindley, London, 1955, pp. 65–6). The 'Chief of Police' no longer appears in the expanded version of the novel published in 1954.

5 Adorno is referring to the remarks on modern city-dwellers in the second volume (1922) of Oswald Spengler's most important work, *Der Untergang des Abendlandes* [The Decline of the West]. See the chapter on 'The Soul of the City' and Adorno's comments in 'Spengler nach dem Untergang', *GS* 10.1, p. 49f.; English translation: 'Spengler after the Decline', in *Prisms*, trans. Samuel Weber and Shierry Weber, London, 1969, p. 55f.

6 Peter Suhrkamp (1891–1959) became the editor of the Berlin journal *Neue Rundschau* in 1933 (published by S. Fischer) and headed the Berlin branch of the publisher from 1936 (which appeared from 1942 under the name Suhrkamp-Verlag, formerly S. Fischer). As a result of disagreements with Gottfried Bermann Fischer (1897–1995), who had emigrated, and transferred the main branch of the original publishing house, to the United States via Vienna and Stockholm in 1936, Peter Suhrkamp founded his own publishing house in Frankfurt in 1950 (and secured the collaboration of a number of authors, such as Hermann Hesse, who had formerly been published by Fischer). On 26 April 1950 the parties finally concluded an agreement 'which was designed, according to the preamble of the contract, both to "re-establish S. Fischer Verlag in its original form and to continue Peter Suhrkamp's publishing venture as the Peter Suhrkamp Verlag"' (Thomas Mann, *Briefwechsel mit seinem Verleger Gottfried Bermann Fischer 1932–1955*, ed. by Peter de Mendelssohn, Frankfurt am Main, 1973, p. 811n.). The authors who had stayed with Peter Suhrkamp in 1936 were subsequently free to negotiate with whichever publishing house they preferred.

7 The poet Friedrich Podszus (1899–1971) was employed as a reader for Suhrkamp Verlag between 1950 and 1956. After the war he published two volumes of verse, *Der Freund der Erde* [The Friend of the Earth] (Munich, 1946) and *Kinderszenen* [Scenes from Childhood] (Munich, 1974). In 1955 he collaborated with Theodor and Gretel Adorno on a two-volume edition of Walter Benjamin's *Writings* for Suhrkamp Verlag.

8 See Adorno, 'Zur Philosophie Husserls', *Archiv für Philosophie*, 3 (1951), pp. 339–78; *GS* 5, pp. 190–235 (the text had been completed in 1938 and subsequently appeared in book form in 1956 as the fourth and final chapter of Adorno's *Zur Metakritik der Erkenntnistheorie* (English translation: *Against Epistemology*, trans. Willis Domingo, Oxford, 1982).

9 See Theodor W. Adorno, 'Auferstehung der Kultur in Deutschland', *Frankfurter Hefte*, 5 (1950), pp. 469–77; *GS* 20.2, pp. 453–64, under the slightly different title 'Die auferstandene Kultur'. Max Rychner (1897–1965) edited the literary features section of the Swiss newspaper *Die Tat* from 1939 onwards. Rychner was a personal friend of Thomas Mann and had already published a number of essays and pieces on his work. He had edited the *Neue Schweizer Rundschau* in the 1920s and acted as the special correspondent in Germany for the *Neue Zürcher Zeitung* between 1933 and 1937. Rychner

printed the opening section of Adorno's radio talk in *Die Tat* and added the
following comments of his own:

> It is particularly instructive to consider Adorno's remarks about the way
> in which the outside world sees the current cultural and intellectual scene
> in Germany: 'one assumes that stupidity, ignorance, and cynical mistrust
> of everything intellectual prevail . . . There is nothing, so one concludes,
> really happening there.' But who assumes this? Who concludes this?
> 'One' does so. Yet this 'one' is a German who grew up in Germany, who
> taught and lived there, who thoroughly studied the sciences of human
> society there with 'keen endeavour' [like Faust]. . . . The result of this
> scholarly endeavour is that a man so well instructed in contemporary
> sociology could adopt as his own the most primitive propagandistic
> clichés that have been 'formed in the world outside'. Now he is back
> inside the country, he suddenly realizes they are not actually true. 'Outside
> Germany one imagines that the barbaric Hitler regime has left nothing
> but barbarism behind. . . . one imagines the destruction of all culture . . .
> But there is no question of this.'
> What a noble confession of error! This is, especially among intellectu-
> als, something as rare as diamonds. It is quite possible that some may
> draw instruction from his example and be prompted to think more care-
> fully about *inside* and *outside* in this respect than they may have done
> before [. . . .] Adorno has furnished us with an example of intellectual
> honesty which can only prove an encouraging source of strength. (Max
> Rychner, 'Auferstehung der Kultur in Deutschland: Zeugnis eines zurück-
> gekehrten Emigranten', *Die Tat* (20 May 1950), p. 11)

10 The premises of the re-established Institute for Social Research were for-
mally opened on 14 November 1951. The Office of the United States High
Commissioner for Germany (HICOG) had expressed considerable interest
in the possibility of pursuing specific sociological research into the political
consciousness of the German population as a whole. Among other things,
the office initiated the 'Darmstadt Studies' and supported the institute in
1950 with a grant of 200,000 Deutschmarks, which funded the first major
piece of research undertaken by the institute after the war (see Letter 19
below, note 3). Before the establishment of a specific UNESCO Institute
for the Social Sciences in Cologne in 1951, there had been some thought of
affiliating such an institution with the Institute for Social Research in
Frankfurt.

11 See Georg Lukács, *Der junge Hegel: Über die Beziehungen von Dialektik
und Ökonomie* (Zürich and Vienna, 1948); English translation: *The Young
Hegel: Studies in the Relations between Dialectics and Economics*, trans.
R. Livingstone (London, 1975).

12 See Lukács's essay 'Reification and the Consciousness of the Proletariat'
in his book *Geschichte und Klassenbewusstsein*, published in Berlin in 1923;
English translation: *History and Class Consciousness: Studies in Marxist
Dialectics*, trans. R. Livingstone (London, 1971), pp. 83–222.

13 See Martin Heidegger, *Holzwege* (Frankfurt am Main, 1950), which contains the essay 'Hegel's Concept of Experience'; English translation: *Hegel's Concept of Experience*, trans. J. Glenn Gray (New York, 1970).

14 A wine particularly prized by Engelbert and Felix Krull in Mann's *Confessions of Felix Krull* (GW VII, pp. 278 and 326; English translation: *Confessions of Felix Krull, Confidence Man: Memoirs Part I*, trans. D. Lindley, London, 1955, p. 20 and p. 69).

18   THOMAS MANN TO THEODOR W. ADORNO
      ZURICH, 1.7.1950

DOLDER GRAND HOTEL
ZÜRICH
1 July 1950

Dear Dr Adorno,

I feel somewhat wretched, after receiving your letter of 3 June, for having had to respond with a pre-printed card[1] which must, inevitably under the circumstances, have sounded rather foolish. In fact my entire correspondence has gone to pieces of late – not simply because of the little celebration[2] which I certainly do not regret having had over here (an affair of quality and cordiality throughout), but primarily on account of my wife's operation[3] – the necessity for which they had concealed from me during the festivities and which was then performed immediately afterwards in the Hirslanden Clinic. 'One of those things', as they say, but no small matter at her age with the possibility of arterial complications and the danger of an embolism and other such horrors. The business had been somewhat delayed, she was in a poor state of nerves generally, and the highly esteemed surgeon, Prof. Traugott,[4] was rather worried about the outcome. But everything went well in the end, and now after the first few days, when the pain was hard to bear, indeed *un*bearable, because she was not initially permitted any pain relief, the process of healing and recuperation has properly begun. And thank goodness – for I was very anxious throughout. The convalescent will be allowed back in about ten days' time, and we shall spend the next three weeks in Sils Maria, where I am sure the mountain air will prove most beneficial.

I have been really thrown off course by events – I should like to complete 'The Chosen One', although I do not take it that seriously, but still lack that inner composure which I need for developing ideas. And the political situation hardly helps one's distracted nerves. Wild horses would not drag me to Germany. I find the spirit of the country objectionable and this mixture of wretchedness and insolence on the basis of excellent prospects quite repulsive. It is a privileged child in the world. America stands in the background, the Schumann Plan[5] is simply an imported project for a German Europe under American protection, under her apron strings for the moment but not in the longer term. The threat of war comes from *there*, not from Korea,[6] which is a nonentity. Russia is hardly engaged, and since we are the ones who are, it now comes down to money whether Russia, after Berlin, will have to suffer another setback.[7] We are sure that Russia does not want war, but they are not so sure about us, and this is a great advantage on our part. But it is also possible that South Korea, where no one wants to fight, will be occupied within ten days, creating a fait accompli to which we shall have to respond by guaranteeing the defence of other places like Formosa or Indo-China. I do not believe there is a danger of war because the Russians know the precise limits of how far they can go – not as far as Persia or West Germany for example.

Your remarks about the country[8] where you now live and work followed the pro-German line rather too closely – or so it seemed. I knew how to interpret them, but so did Rychner. Best wishes for your vital tight-rope dance in this respect, and for mine!

Yours,
Thomas Mann

SOURCE: O: MS with printed hotel letterhead; Theodor W. Adorno Archive, Frankfurt am Main. Pp: *DüD*, p. 369.

1 The card, dated Zurich, 8 June 1950, which Adorno was sent, has not survived, but one is preserved in the Thomas Mann Archive. It reads as follows: 'You are among those who have remembered me so cordially on my seventy-fifth birthday with fair and encouraging words, with splendid flowers, with lovely gifts of every kind. I am overcome by such kindness and can here only express my thanks with a card which I hope you will receive not as a formal manifestation of coolness, but as a quite personally intended and personally directed expression of deeply felt gratitude on my part, Thomas Mann'

2 Letter 20 below, note 10.

3 Katia Mann had to enter the Hirslanden Clinic in Zurich for a gynaecological operation in June 1950. Although there were no surgical complications, she remained in hospital for at least a month.

4 The gynaecologist Marcel Traugott (1882–1961), who operated on Katia Mann, had left Germany and emigrated to Switzerland in 1933. He had practised in Zurich since 1935 (see Thomas Mann, *Tagebücher 1949–1950*, pp. 200–3, 210f., 245 and 560n.).

5 The French foreign minister Robert Schumann (1886–1963) was attempting to encourage economic co-operation between France and Germany in the coal and steel industry, with the ultimate intention of establishing a Common

European Market. 'In an interview published in the Stockholm communist newspaper *Ny Dag*, Thomas Mann described this plan as "very dangerous for France": "Schumann has still not understood the psychology of the Germans. I fear that he is really deluding himself about the great industrial barons of the Ruhrgebiet. They are not remotely interested in genuine co-operation, but only in their own power. There is a danger, therefore, that France will become little more than a province of the German economy, and this would effectively force France off the stage entirely"' (see Thomas Mann, *Tagebücher 1949–1950*, p. 553).

6 North Korean troops had crossed the line of demarcation on 24–25 June 1950 and had begun to occupy the territory of the South. American troops were mobilized to support South Korea on 27 June. The Soviet Union had demanded reunification of both parts of the country. The Korean War was ended only in 1953, and the political division of the peninsula has remained in force ever since.

7 Thomas Mann is probably alluding back to the attempted Russian blockade of Berlin and the ensuing allied airlift between July 1948 and May 1949. He may also have been thinking of the large pro-Western demonstrations in West Berlin in May 1950 and the publicly expressed decision of the three Western occupying powers to revise the original Occupation Agreement and retain a continuing presence in Berlin.

8 Thomas Mann is referring to Adorno's radio talk 'Die Auferstehung der Kultur in Deutschland' [The Resurrection of Culture in Germany]. In printing the opening section of Adorno's talk in *Die Tat* (see Letter 17 above), Max Rychner had emphasized the following remark: 'The relationship to the things of the mind, in the broadest sense, is strong. It seems to me to be greater than it was in the years before the National Socialists seized political power', although he made no further attempt to analyse it. Thomas Mann is probably alluding to this emphasis, and to Adorno's remarks about his positive impressions of university life and the 'intellectual passion' of the students.

19   THEODOR W. ADORNO TO THOMAS MANN
      FRANKFURT AM MAIN, 6.7.1950

Liebigstr. 19[III]
Frankfurt/Main

6 July 1950

My dear and esteemed Dr Mann,
   I was very disturbed to learn of your wife's recent illness and operation. It had not escaped either of us that she had been suffering health problems for some while, but the specific news still came as a shock. And I feel all the happier now to hear that everything has gone well. Please do pass on to your dear patient our best wishes for her speedy

and complete recovery. I can easily and clearly imagine what it must have been like for you during the period of the operation. One of the most terrible things in such situations is just the feeling of one's own helplessness, the shadow of that very division of labour to which alone medicine nonetheless owes its triumphs.

I feel rather envious to hear that you will be in Sils Maria, and God knows not simply on account of the aura of the place, but because I can myself still physically recall the literally magical air of the Engadine. I hope it may stay as vividly in the memory for both of you as that 'two thousand meters high above the sea, let alone human beings'.[1] I actually thought that you had finished 'The Chosen One' in the meantime – perhaps the Engadine will be good for him too. For our part, we cannot even think of taking a holiday at present, although we have both certainly more than earned one. But the semester lasts until 1 August, and then we hope to move into our apartment,[2] which is a homely and attractive place. It takes a lot of effort to arrange all this, although it also involves more agreeable things like trying to acquire a Steinway piano. There is a sociological congress in Zurich planned for the beginning of September.[3] Either Horkheimer or I, and perhaps both of us, will certainly put in an appearance and proffer a few words of wisdom. Will you still be here on shared ground? If so, you will surely not escape a sudden visitation.

You will be diverted to learn that we still maintain very cordial relations with Bermann-Fischer,[4] as if I had never done anything to offend. We were invited round to his place the evening before yesterday, and your ears must have been ringing. He has succeeded in acquiring the German publishing rights for Kafka's work, and he has asked me to deliver the opening lecture at a public reading[5] – obviously an impossible task in its way, but one that attracts me nonetheless; and I already have a good excuse for daring to undertake such a thing: it is required if only to ward off something worse, like the kind of interpretation offered by Brod or Schöps.[6] This *événement* is not expected to take place until the end of the autumn.

I am slightly troubled by your own impression that my remarks 'rather supported the pro-German line', and even more so by the suggestion that Rychner also knew how to interpret them – which implies an ambiguity to my radio lecture which was entirely unintended. In the lecture, which actually appeared in the *Frankfurter Hefte* with countless minor unauthorized changes of language which taken together nonetheless conspired to vulgarize the totality of the piece, I was merely attempting to clarify the experience which has accompanied the course of my recent work. I should not have underestimated that positive phenomenon that is often described, with an admittedly very suspect expression, as 'spiritual passion'. But as a confirmed dialectician I simply included it as a thesis which immanently implies the suspect idea of self-certain spirit as its own antithesis. I believed that the negative side was so overwhelmingly expressed, that the positive beginning could simply perform the role of a *captatio benevolentiae*. My literary abilities have obviously proved insufficient in this respect. Nonetheless I am pained by Herr Rychner's sympathetic interpretation of my words. For now I should simply insist that no one may deny us the right to think dialectically about contemporary Germany too, and I am quite sure that you will agree with me in this.

I share your view that there is no immediate danger of war. Certainly not from the Russian side, and nor from the American side – if only because a preventive war would require the kind of total mobilization which the Truman administration,[7] for all the current outcry, is not prepared to undertake. I do not think I have a sufficiently clear picture concerning the full background of the Schumann plan. I regard the danger of encouraging German hegemony as rather less serious than you do because I have been increasingly struck by the prevailing feeling of rupture and inner brokenness here, and because it really seems to me that German nationalism has overreached itself by the cruel pitch of its own extremity. The wretched aspect which you emphasize implies that the Germans wish to attach themselves to the great current constellations of power in order to secure some tangible advantages for themselves in the present – the hope of successfully asserting themselves once again as an imperialistic 'subject' has entirely vanished. But perhaps I am regarding all of this rather too much from the perspective of individuals, insofar as the role of Germany is anyway objectively determined by global political factors beyond the conscious control of the inhabitants. And the industrialists of the Ruhr are still much the same as they were before, as I could observe for myself during a recent trip to Dortmund.[8]

That our own dear Hans Mayer,[9] in his book about you, has identified me as the literal model for your Devil, with whom I have little in common beyond the horn-rimmed spectacles, will have astonished you as much as it has me – for I have certainly never been aware of possessing such diabolical characteristics. I should also mention that an extremely capable lecturer by the name of Josef Kunz,[10] someone who is devoted to your work, has been giving three hour-long lectures about you at the university, and they have proved a great success with the students here. It would give you considerable pleasure to meet this decent and intelligent man sometime.

Since my vanity will not tolerate your numbering me even temporarily among the *boches*, I feel obliged to include here the manuscript of an essay on Walter Benjamin[11] which the *Neue Rundschau* invited me to compose on the occasion of the tenth anniversary of his death. I hope there will be no further problems about them publishing the piece. This is the only thing of my own I have been able to produce during the last few months.

I should be extremely grateful for any response and remain, as always, cordially and devotedly yours,

[Teddie Adorno]

SOURCE: O: TS (carbon copy); Theodor W. Adorno Archive, Frankfurt am Main.

1 On 3 September 1883 Nietzsche wrote, from Sils Maria, to Heinrich Köselitz: 'This Engadine is the birth-place of my Zarathustra. I have just come across the first sketch of the ideas which are expressed there. Underneath I read: "Beginning of August 1881 in Sils Maria, 6000 feet above the sea and much higher above all human things".' And in *Ecce Homo* Nietzsche also discusses the origin of *Zarathustra*: 'The basic conception of the work [. . .] goes back to the August of 1881: thrown down on a single page with the subscription: "6000 feet beyond mankind and time". That day I walked through the woods along the lake of Silvaplana [. . .]' A formulation that is the same as Adorno's 'citation' has not been identified.

2 In the Frankfurt Westend: Kettenhofweg 123.

3 A conference of the re-established 'International Sociological Association' (ISA) took place in Zurich on 4–5 September 1950. There is no evidence that Adorno and/or Horkheimer actually participated in the event.

4 Adorno is referring to his decision to publish his work with Suhrkamp, although Thomas Mann had already attempted to interest Bermann Fischer in the idea of publishing Adorno's *Minima Moralia*.

5 Adorno's lecture was probably prompted by the publication of *The Trial*, in volume 1 of the second edition of Kafka's works published by Max Brod between 1950 and 1958. No further details about the lecture in question have been discovered.

6 In 1931 Max Brod (1884–1968) and Hans-Joachim Schoeps (1909–1980) had already published a volume, entitled *Franz Kafka: Beim Bau der chinesischen Mauer*, which contained previously unpublished materials from Kafka's literary remains. Both commentators, but especially Brod, had defended a religiously oriented interpretation of Kafka. See Max Brod's biography of Kafka (Prague, 1937) and his book *Franz Kafkas Glauben und Lehren* [The Faith and Doctrine of Franz Kafka], published in 1948; and H.–J. Schoeps's essay 'Theologische Motive in der Dichtung Franz Kafkas' [Theological Themes in the Work of Franz Kafka], *Neue Rundschau*, 1 (1951).

7 Harry S Truman (1884–1972), vice-president in 1945, became the thirty-third president of the United States after the death of Franklin D. Roosevelt later in the same year. On 2 December 1948 he was re-elected by the Democratic Party as their presidential candidate.

8 At the end of May and the beginning of June 1950 Adorno visited the research institute based at the University of Münster in order to organize and prepare for the first research programme to be undertaken by the re-established Institute for Social Research (see *Gruppenexperiment: Ein Studienbericht*, ed. Friedrich Pollock, *Frankfurter Beiträge zur Soziologie*, Vol. 2, Frankfurt am Main, 1955). There was another meeting to analyse and discuss the research material in Frankfurt at the end of June and the beginning of July. At this time there were clearly plans for close collaboration between the Institute of Social Research and the research institute in Münster – see Letter 21, note 1.

9 In his book *Thomas Mann: Werk und Entwicklung* [Thomas Mann: His Work and Development] (Berlin, 1950), Hans Mayer describes the different faces which the Devil reveals to Adrian Leverkühn in the course of *Doctor Faustus*: 'In the meantime, in the great dialogue which turns upon the fate of music, of modern art in general, he has changed appearance once again. The Devil now sports the horn-rimmed spectacles of the intellectual, and thereby strikes Leverkühn much more sympathetically than before. The transitory earthly form which Thomas Mann has faithfully bestowed upon him here is another cause for wonder on the part of the reader. Unless we are much mistaken, Leverkühn's partner in dialogue now assumes the features of the remarkable theoretician of music whom Thomas Mann so tirelessly consulted as the "real privy councillor" for the musical parts of the book. It is a portrait of Theodor W. Adorno' (ibid., p. 370).

10 The literary historian Joseph Kunz (*b.* 1906) had delivered lectures on 'Problems of Genre in relation to the Novel' in the winter semester of 1948–9, and on 'The Structure of the German Novella' in the summer of 1949. Kunz was appointed extraordinary professor in Frankfurt am Main in 1951 and called to Marburg an der Lahn as full professor in 1959.

11 See Adorno, 'Charakteristik Walter Benjamins', *Neue Rundschau*, 61 (1950), pp. 571–84; *GS* 10.1, pp. 238–53; English translation: 'A Portrait of Walter Benjamin', in *Prisms*, trans. Samuel Weber and Shierry Weber (London, 1967), pp. 227–41.

20   THOMAS MANN TO THEODOR W. ADORNO
     ZURICH, 11.7.1950

DOLDER GRAND HOTEL
ZÜRICH
11 July 1950

Dear Dr Adorno,
  No offence intended! I told you that I knew how to read your essay. If Rychner was also capable of reading and interpreting the piece in his own way, this derives from his 'positive' prejudice in favour of re-immigration itself, of the very decision to live and work in Germany.

These Swiss conservatives are friendly to the Germans and hostile to the idea of emigration, and they will praise everything that promotes reconciliation and military withdrawal. If it is not exactly what the text says, they will read this into it anyway – and the *Frankfurter Hefte*,[1] a publication that regularly denigrates and insults me in the best new German fashion, seems to have played into Rychner's hands here with its little stylistic modifications and simplifications of expression. For the rest, R is not only an essayist of some quality, but a genuine creative writer. He has recently published an epyllion, 'The First Ones',[2] a poetic trialogue between Adam, Eve and the Serpent which is an undeniably beautiful piece. Everything thus seems to have two sides to it. I would not gladly lose you to the Germans, but I very much share the desire that you will actually be able to exercise an active influence there. Accept my best wishes for when you move into your comfortable new apartment, not to mention the Steinway. But I should also like to know more about the academic prospects where you are. You will surely never become an Ordinarius![3] But then how are things in America in this respect? How often we turned our thoughts to *leaving* that country. Who would have entertained the idea, only three years ago, of now undertaking a second emigration?

Your essay on Benjamin has proved to be *fascinating* reading for me, and it was an intelligent move on Bermann's part to engage you for the lecture on Kafka. For who is better fitted than you to speak about Kafka in this context? I think the word *événement*, which you intend ironically, is in fact entirely appropriate.

Kafka loved my 'Tonio Kröger'[4] – that is *one* memory among others (Hofmannsthal, Schnitzler, Beer-Hofmann,[5] Hesse, even Hauptmann) which contradicts Hans Mayer's remarks on the lack of any real rapport between my own work and that of other contemporary writers and on my role as an 'unappealing' figure in this regard.[6] There are certainly many perceptive insights in his book for which one should be grateful, but also significant omissions and irrelevancies, and the idea that my musically schooled Devil is specifically drawn after your own image is absurd in the extreme. Do you ever wear horn-rimmed spectacles? There is certainly no other trace of similarity to be found here. But people are always anxious to 'notice' as much as possible in these matters.

I have to ask myself whether such a book is really helpful, is really capable of decisively identifying the true path of a life across the spiritual firmament. But I have expressed my faith in this possibility to the author and thanked him for all his efforts.[7] But I have recently been reading in Spitteler about how much, and how much of any depth, has been written about Viktor Scheffel,[8] whom Spitteler himself admired enormously. One must just carry on without really knowing how things will turn out. And in the last analysis it can all seem so irrelevant anyway. Extravagant confessions of love and idiotic denunciations are both equally tedious to me. I doubt that Lecturer Kunz will figure any more prominently in my letters than the 'perceptive Dane Dr Georg Brandes' and his lectures featured in those of Nietzsche.[9]

I must say that I have no regrets about arranging to have my little celebration over here. It was all a very cordial and distinguished affair – with speeches by Strich, Helbling and de Salis for example.[10] 'The benevolence of our contemporaries', as Goethe said, 'is indeed at last a proven joy.'[11] And there is a greater spark of life in my 'Faustus', I believe, than there is in 'The Trumpeter of Säckingen'.[12]

My most heartfelt regards to you and your dear wife. I am looking forward to reading the Benjamin piece for the third time once it appears in the *Rundschau*. 'All of his observations are equally close to the centre'[13] – this strongly reminded me of Schopenhauer, who no more respected the distinction between philosophical text and essay form than did Nietzsche. I would change the remark about the 'exceptionwise character of his nature' since 'wise' here is effectively an adverb. If one does not want to refer to his 'exceptionality', I suppose we must simply speak of his 'excepting' or 'exceptional' nature.

Yours,

Thomas Mann

We are leaving for Sils Maria on Saturday
What about saying: 'The exceptional side to his nature'?

SOURCE: O: MS with printed hotel letterhead; Theodor W. Adorno Archive, Frankfurt am Main. Fp: *Briefe III*, p. 158f.

1 Mann is obviously referring to pieces such as Ulrich Sonnenmann's essay 'Thomas Mann oder Anspruch und Maß' (see *Frankfurter Hefte: Zeitschrift für Kultur und Politik*, 3 (1948), pp. 625–40 and Erich Kuby's contribution 'Der fünfundsiebzigjährige Thomas Mann' (ibid., 5 (1950), pp. 643–5, or remarks such as those of Maida Delbrück in 'Eine Frau liest Thomas Mann' (ibid., 4 (1949), p. 620f.).

2 See Max Rychner, *Die Ersten: Ein Epyllion* (Zurich, 1949).

3 Adorno was made unofficial extraordinary professor in 1950, official extraordinary professor in 1953, and finally ordinary professor of philosophy in 1956 in Frankfurt am Main.

4 In 1904 Franz Kafka had written to Max Brod, who was considering sending a copy of his own novella *Ausflug ins Dunkelrothe* to Thomas Mann: 'I am surprised that you have written nothing to me about Tonio Kröger. But I said to myself: "He knows how happy I am to receive a letter from him, and he will have to say something about Tonio Kröger. He clearly must have written to me, but then there are always accidents, storms, earthquakes, and

his letter has never arrived" [. . .] Perhaps you will also write to me about the similarities to your own story 'Ausflug ins Dunkelrothe'. I had indeed already reflected upon this far-reaching similarity between them even before recently re-reading 'Tonio Kröger'. For what is so new about 'Tonio Kröger' is not the discovery of this opposition [namely between 'life' and 'art'] (and thank God that I no longer have to believe in this, truly intimidating, opposition), but rather the peculiar, and beneficial, infatuation with opposition itself (like the writer in "Ausflug")' (Franz Kafka, *Briefe 1900–1912*, ed. Hans-Gerd Koch, Frankfurt am Main, 1999, p. 41f.). On 6 June 1925, Thomas Mann's fiftieth birthday, Max Brod had written in the *Berliner Tageblatt*: 'I hope he will permit me, on this happy day of his, to recall one of the saddest of my own, to link this living writer with a dead one, with Franz Kafka. For I have always perceived Thomas Mann through the infinitely loving and lovingly respectful medium of my friend, who prized few contemporary authors as fervently as he did Thomas Mann. He read every single one of his works with excitement. This became a true significant event in his life' (Thomas Mann, *Briefwechsel mit Autoren*, ed. Hans Wysling, Frankfurt am Main, 1988, p. 79).

5 The Austrian writer and dramatist Richard Beer-Hofmann (1866–1945), with Hugo von Hofmannsthal (1874–1929) and Arthur Schnitzler (1862–1931), belonged to the circle of 'Young Vienna'. Beer-Hofmann was known mainly for the poem 'Schlaflied für Mirjam' (1919), and his principal work, the verse trilogy *Die Historie von König David*, was left unfinished at his death. Thomas Mann had met the writer in Vienna in 1919. Beer-Hofmann emigrated to the United States via Zurich in 1938 and died in New York in 1945.

6 See Hans Mayer, *Thomas Mann: Werk und Entwicklung* [Thomas Mann: His Work and Development] (Berlin, 1950). In the chapter entitled 'Gerhart Hauptmann oder die Persönlichkeit' (pp. 163–82) Mayer had spoken of the 'distance' and the 'cool attitude displayed by almost every contemporary writer towards Thomas Mann as man and writer' (ibid., p. 172), explicitly referring among others to Hofmannsthal, George, Rilke, Kafka, Brecht, Musil and Arnold Zweig. 'Thomas Mann was unattractive to them all' (ibid., p. 173).

7 In his letter to Hans Mayer on 23 June 1950 Thomas Mann had written: 'I cannot, and need not, say how grateful I am to you for the spirited way in which you have immersed yourself in my life's work, for the way you have depicted it as a kind of constellation' (*Briefe III*, p. 154).

8 See Carl Spitteler, 'Viktor Scheffel', in *Gesammelte Werke*, ed. Gottfried Bohnenblust, Wilhelm Altwegg and Robert Faesi, Vol. 9: *Aus der Werkstatt*, ed. Werner Stauffacher (Zurich, 1950), pp. 314–16.

9 The Danish literary historian Georg Brandes (1842–1927) had lectured on Nietzsche at the University of Copenhagen in 1888, something which Nietzsche frequently mentions in his correspondence during the summer of 1888 (see letters to Meta von Salis of 17 June 1888, to Karl Kortz of 21 June 1883, to Carl Fuchs of 29 July 1888, and to Malwida von Meysenbug of the

end of July 1888). Nietzsche refers to 'the perceptive Dane Dr Georg Brandes' in his letter to Ernst Wilhelm Fritsch of May 1888.

10 See Jean Rodolphe von Salis, 'Thomas Mann zum 6 Juni 1950', in *Im Lauf der Jahre: Über Geschichte, Politik und Literatur* (Zurich, 1962), pp. 302–8. The other commemorative speeches, delivered by the literary historians Carl Helbling (1897–1966) and Fritz Strich (1882–1963), do not appear to have been published. A tape recording of the speech by Fritz Strich, and of that by Richard Schweizer (1900–1965), has been preserved in the Thomas Mann Archive.

11 Mann is quoting the concluding lines of Goethe's late poem with the superscription '28 August 1826'.

12 A verse epic of 1854 by Josef Victor von Scheffel (1826–1886).

13 Adorno's exact wording was: 'All of his observations are equally near to the centre' (*GS* 10.1, p. 242; English translation: *Prisms*, London, 1969, p. 232).

21   THEODOR W. ADORNO TO THOMAS MANN
     FRANKFURT AM MAIN, 1.8.1950

Frankfurt, 1 August 1950

Dear and esteemed Dr Mann,

Please forgive me for taking so long to reply to your letter. The end of the current semester has brought with it a massive amount of work, including participation in a conference of sociologists in the Ruhrgebiet.[1] I actually shared the platform with the director – and having become a real expert on the financial details of the administration in Witten can now identify most emphatically with Krull. May my own good thoughts help in bringing his birth to pass.

It is a weight off my chest to know that you do not hold me responsible for Rychner's warm endorsement of my words. Yesterday evening Horkheimer and I were discussing a plan to bring out a volume, with Gadamer, on Nietzsche.[2] We shall attempt to correct the nonsensical situation that Nietzsche is widely regarded abroad as the ancestral father of fascism, while over here they prefer to trivialize him into a kind of Jaspers figure. Are you aware, incidentally, that efforts are already being made to reopen Bayreuth?[3] And have you considered taking any steps to oppose the idea? Max von Brück, who is clearly a man of integrity, has just sent me an article on the subject which appeared in 'Die Gegenwart'.[4] It strikes me that the issue of Bayreuth, together with the lifting of Heidegger's teaching ban,[5] is one of the most troubling symptoms of a reluctance to address directly the central problems involved here.

I understand your thoughts on the possibility of a second emigration only too well, but where would you go? You would probably be able to lead a less disturbed life over there within a framework that is already familiar, and that is something that can hardly be overestimated as far as the continuous progress of one's work is concerned. We feel a tremendous longing for the Pacific, which may not be Korea, yet nonetheless deserves its peaceful name in comparison with how things stand over here. But the state of the world suggests that it is almost irrelevant where one actually lives – it seems wisest to allow oneself to be governed by the given possibilities of the moment. I also feel a profound inner resistance against the idea of taking measures to try and ensure one's own safety in the case of atomic war. If the end actually threatens, then one should at least be there. But then you know that I do not believe this really will transpire.

You were kind enough to enquire about my current academic situation. They have just made me an ordinary professor and have now also offered me an honorary professorship. I haven't accepted the latter because, if we actually stay here in the long term, I should prefer to be offered a chair. As things stand at present I am on the list, with a couple of others, as a possible successor to Gadamer in Scheler's old chair.[6] Whether it will work out is obviously quite uncertain, but there is no opposition to the idea here at the university. If it all comes to nothing, then 'that's the way it is', as they say in Berlin. In the meantime Horkheimer has been elected dean.[7]

I am very proud to learn that you liked my piece on Benjamin. I am sure I hardly need to say that I had thought of you as the ideal reader of this essay. In the meantime Suhrkamp has decided to bring out Benjamin's previously unpublished 'A Berlin Childhood' in book form, with Gretel as editor.[8] There is also no longer any doubt that *Minima Moralia* will appear, although I fear the publication will now be delayed until early next year. Unfortunately Suhrkamp is playing around with the idea of inserting a subtitle like 'a philosophy of everyday life' or something similar,[9] to which I am profoundly opposed – but my head will surely prove hard enough to shatter all hopes and plans of this kind.

Anyone who assumes, in seriousness, the responsibility of writing about you cannot content himself with crudely extracting what you, with the deepest delicacy, have hidden in your work, but must rather expose what the work itself has hidden. And this would have to be interpretation in the philosophical sense, not some commentary on the philosophical content. And such a formidable task can really instruct one in the meaning of fear – but our good friend Mayer has unfortunately never experienced this fear, not even before himself, let alone before the Devil. It is wretched that in matters of the spirit, where truth is actually at stake, a merely good and well-meaning approach like this accomplishes absolutely nothing.

I have already corrected the expression to which you objected in the essay on Benjamin and replaced 'exception-wise' with 'incommensurable'. I am not wholly satisfied with this either. Your criticism here has brought home to me all the more clearly the writer's dilemma: one either defers to the tact of language, which almost inevitably involves a loss of precision in the matter, or one privileges the latter over the former and thereby does violence to language itself. Every sentence is effectively an aporia, and every successful utterance a happy deliverance, a realization of the impossible, a reconciliation of subjective intention with objective spirit, whereas the essence consists precisely in the diremption of both.

But your words of endorsement have encouraged me to send you a piece on Husserl[10] which I composed ten years ago, and which has just appeared in the *Archiv für Philosophie*. The discussion is largely confined to the characteristic issues of official epistemology, but carried out in a rather aggressive manner – it is an attempt to break with idealism in an immanent way precisely by pursuing the consequences of its own dialectic. Basically the task is not to confront philosophy with dialectical materialism in an external and dogmatic fashion, but rather to grasp this materialism as the very truth of philosophy in its objectivity. That this has never properly been done before, I am convinced, is in large part responsible for what has become of Marxism. If you read the work with these thoughts in the background, you may be able to forgive the terminological armourplating on the outside and discover a Brünhilde within – who was also originally conceived as a liberating figure of course.

Hopefully you have both entirely recovered by now and felt that joy at the view of Palü and Bernina[11] which the most perfect of all mountains, with its utterly unique site, can alone vouchsafe.

The best of greetings to you both, from Gretel too,
Your cordially devoted,
Teddie Adorno

SOURCE: O: TS with handwritten corrections; Thomas Mann Archive, Zurich.

1 The conference took place in Witten, near Dortmund, on 21 and 22 July 1950 at the invitation of the Social Research Centre of the University of Münster (based in Dortmund).

2 See Theodor W. Adorno, Max Horkheimer and Hans-Georg Gadamer, 'Über Nietzsche und uns: Zum 50. Todestag des Philosophen', in Max Horkheimer, *Gesammelte Schriften*, Vol. 13: *Nachgelassene Schriften*

1949–1972, ed. Gunzelin Schmid Noerr, Frankfurt am Main, 1989, pp. 111–20.

3 The first Bayreuth Festival after the end of the war opened on 29 June 1951.

4 See Max von Brück, 'Es geht um Wagner' [Wagner is the Question], *Die Gegenwart* (15 June 1950), p. 9f.

5 The philosopher Martin Heidegger (1889–1976) had been banned from academic teaching between 1945 and 1951. There had been a number of attempts since 1949 to permit him to return to the University of Freiburg.

6 Hans-Georg Gadamer (1900–2004) had occupied the former chair of Max Scheler (1874–1928) in Frankfurt since 1947. He was offered a professorship in Heidelberg in 1949. As possible successors to Gadamer the Faculty of Philosophy in Frankfurt had suggested, on 6 July 1950, the names of Josef König (Hamburg), Gerhard Krüger (Tübingen) and Adorno. Gerhard Krüger was offered the professorship in Frankfurt in 1952 (see Letter 20, note 3, above).

7 Max Horkheimer was elected dean of the Faculty of Philosophy on 4 July 1950.

8 The first edition of Walter Benjamin's text *A Berlin Childhood around 1900*, edited by Gretel Adorno, appeared in Frankfurt in 1950. See W. Benjamin, *Gesammelte Schriften*, ed. Rolf Tiedemann and Hermann Schweppenhäuser, with the collaboration of Theodor W. Adorno and Gershom Scholem, Vol. IV.1, ed. Tillmann Rexroth, Frankfurt am Main, 1991, pp. 235–304.

9 The subtitle which Adorno eventually chose was 'Reflections from Damaged Life'.

10 See Letter 17, note 8, below.

11 Thomas Mann stayed in Sils Maria and St Moritz between 15 July and 8 August 1950.

IFENHOTEL
HIRSCHEGG
BEI OBERSDORF ALLG.
KL. WALSERTAL
BES. HANS KIRCHHOFF
TEL. RIEZLERN 23

Hirschegg, 25 Aug. 1951

My dear and esteemed Dr Mann,

I am not sure whether you received my card.[1] We are only here until Tuesday because it now turns out that I really have to leave for Los Angeles as soon as possible.[2] I shall be spending a couple of weeks there from the middle of September. At all events I shall certainly get in touch with you then.

But for now, *procul negotiis*, I should not like to miss the opportunity of saying at least a few words about 'The Chosen One'.[3] I have read it 'like cake'.[4] And perhaps it is no accident that this expression of Keller's occurs to me in this connection since it is surely the tradition of 'The Seven Legends'[5] which you are effectively continuing here in a uniquely oblique manner. By this I mean that the relationship between the ironic treatment and the material itself, just as in Keller, is infinitely more differentiated than it is in the writing of France,[6] or in any simple 'enlightened' reading of inherited myth. For it is not the myth which you treat ironically – rather the irony already lies in the selection of the legendary material itself. And everything surely depends, in deciphering the highly cryptic content of the work – which incidentally I hardly dare to attempt – upon what is really being subjected to irony here. It strikes me that one of the manifold tracks on your map, the one which leads to 'Disorder and Early Grief',[7] has here crossed the path of another, the one that leads to 'Joseph'. I am surely not the only person who feels this work to be something like a requiem for Klaus and the entire state of mind he represents.[8] The legendary element performs a redemptive role here through its own uniquely enchanting remoteness. It is also this theme of redemption which discloses what lies behind the irony. If I am not mistaken this concerns the taboo that weighs upon the thought of incest. The artistic way in which you have handled Christian grace and clemency, itself ironic in dispensing with any unjustifiable trust in the theological promise of salvation, actually says, without quite saying it, that the forbidden deed is perhaps not so terrible at all. The sadly reconciled tone with which the resolution is finally pronounced itself dissolves the deceptive horror of the predicament. One can almost imagine that the fateful power of incest, as Freud described it,[9] fades away at the very moment when it is exposed. The passage where Pope Gregorius vividly evokes for his mother the consequences that would have arisen from his relationship with the children of this marriage[10] has become justly famous; and that the writing here even trusts itself to laugh over the abysmal depths of such kin-relationships clearly allows the theme of redemption to emerge. But I was perhaps even more powerfully struck by the passage in the description of the siblings' night of incestuous love[11] where the narrator relates that the killing of the dog seemed far more reprehensible to him than this incestuous sexuality – something which was enough to make one regret being an only child. If your novel can be described as playful, then only in the most emphatic sense of play, as the play of freedom.

Naturally it does an injustice to a work of art of such quality to try and construe its implicit 'idea' like a proper, and therefore improper, philosopher. The specific detail, which springs creatively from the idea, always outweighs the latter. Here I could simply mention the duel,[12] or the priceless creature Sturmi, which I can now no longer banish from the world of my own thoughts and words, or the scene of penance upon the mountain[13] – and this last especially. You have overcome the impossibility of unfolding such a scene through your truly brilliant mastery of indefinite suggestion, as if everything had been murmured forth in sleep – like the murmuring little creature itself?[14] Again this all belongs perfectly to the whole domain of dreams.

This murmuring aspect, if I am not deceived, relates at the same time to a certain stratum of language, a borderline where the distinguishing feature of language itself begins to vanish. It is as if you had realized here, in your very own material, something resembling the kind of music, gliding back and forth between specific tonal regions, that you had already ascribed to Leverkühn. The boldness and modernity of these things is, if we except Joyce, quite unparalleled, but no less striking is the careful way in which you have managed to suspend the whole 'German' element. It often sounds as though, at a certain decayed level of language, at the level of emigrant German, you had somehow disclosed the latent possibility of a truly European language, one which was formerly obstructed by national divisions but now, at the end, shines forth as a primordial stratum precisely by virtue of its latest character. And this linguistic promiscuity surely stands in the closest relationship to the redemption of incest: it confounds, in the gentlest way, the very order of things. Precisely in the light of your enormously disciplined way with language, such release and abandonment assumes a dignity entirely its own. This is really not so far from certain intentions of the later Schönberg, whose works also display a remarkable sense of liberation, something which in my own terminology I should like to call a critique of authenticity.

I was deeply affected by the news of Schönberg's death[15] – not merely because of the impossibility now of repairing something in a fundamentally difficult relationship, but even more because he was never able, for reasons which are certainly not simply empirical, to bring his two great biblical works[16] to a satisfactory conclusion. Only a few weeks ago I witnessed the first performance of the scene of the Golden Calf,[17] under Scherchen in Darmstadt, which was just like something described in your Faustus novel. This work, which was actually composed twenty years ago, made an enormous impression on me precisely through its power and spontaneity, although the very immediate effect of the piece, in spite of its musical complexity, reveals a latent conservatism – I am not entirely sure whether he has not effectively attempted, albeit brilliantly, to produce some old effects by rather new means. But he has done so, of course, only in an uncommonly sublimated manner, and it is quite possible that I am mistaken here. One can only speak of conservatism in something like the sense in which Schönberg defends it in his last book:[18] that the task of music is to resolve the tensions which it harbours in and through the totality – and this is basically a harmonistic ideal. I can easily imagine that Schönberg's work will one day be described as 'classical music', much as the young quantum physicists of today describe Einstein's work as classical physics. But this classical character, although it may seem to limit the explosive potential of a work, also embodies the highest peak of achievement. I really felt it was a great pity that we were unable to go and listen to this work together. The text, of course, is something that is best shrouded in silence.

May I enquire about your further progress with Krull? And is there any prospect that you might be able to recite some of it for me? I have heard a rumour that your interrupted work on the novel is now explained in the text itself – certainly a most delightful idea.[19]

Fairest greetings to you all, from Gretel too,

Your cordially devoted,

Teddie Adorno

SOURCE: O: TS with printed hotel letterhead; Thomas Mann Archive, Zurich.

1 The card has not survived.

2 Adorno's trip was prompted by the opening of the Hacker Psychiatric Foundation in Beverly Hills. The Austrian psychiatrist and psychoanalyst Frederick Hacker (1914–1989) had emigrated to the United States via Switzerland and Britain in 1938. In the spring of 1950 Hacker was already

planning to turn the psychiatric clinic which he had run since 1945 into a research institute, and was also hoping to establish close academic collaboration with the Institute for Social Research in Frankfurt. He thought that Horkheimer and Adorno, both of whom had given lectures and participated in discussions at his clinic during the 1940s, might be engaged as possible research directors for his new institute. Any extended absence from Frankfurt was impossible for Horkheimer once he had been elected rector of the University of Frankfurt in November 1951. In the autumn of 1952 Adorno returned to Los Angeles for almost a year. For further details on Adorno's work with the Hacker Foundation, see Letter 28 (note 3) below, and the letter from Adorno and Horkheimer to Frederick Hacker of 2 March 1951, in Max Horkheimer, *Gesammelte Schriften*, Vol. 18: *Briefwechsel 1949–1973*, ed. Gunzelin Schmid Noerr, Frankfurt am Main, 1996, pp. 193–8.

3 Thomas Mann's novel *Der Erwählte* (later translated into English as *The Holy Sinner*) was published in 1951 in Frankfurt and New York (to secure the American copyright).

4 Gottfried Keller had used the expression in a letter to Julius Rodenberg of 29 December 1879: 'But Ferdinand Meyer's "Heiliger" is a very beautiful and profound work. If the wonderfully holy Lord himself were not always invisible, I would tell him it is only the very young age of the chancellor's daughter . . . that disturbs me as a difficult and unattractive detail. But otherwise the story reads like cake' (cited from *Gottfried Kellers Leben, Briefe und Tagebücher* (Stuttgart and Berlin, 1915–16), Vol. 3: *Gottfried Kellers Briefe und Tagebücher 1861–1890*, p. 302f.).

5 Gottfried Keller's cycle of *Legends* was published in Stuttgart in 1872.

6 The French writer Anatole France (1844–1924).

7 Adorno is referring to Mann's story 'Unordnung und frühes Leid' of 1925 (see *GW* VIII, pp. 618–57). Mann's tetralogy of novels *Joseph und seine Brüder* had appeared in 1933, 1934, 1936 and 1942; English translation: *Joseph and his Brothers*, trans. H. T. Lowe-Porter (Harmondsworth, 1978).

8 On receiving Adorno's letter Mann wrote in his diary for 1 September 1951: 'Adorno . . . rather strangely perceives some reference to Klaus's fate here.'

9 See above all Freud's essay 'The Inhibition of Incest', which was published with three other essays in the volume *Totem and Taboo* in Vienna in 1913.

10 In the final chapter of the novel, entitled 'The Audience', after the mother's confession, the children Stultitia and Humilitas come forward, and Gregorius says to Sybilla: 'So you see, revered and beloved, and God be praised for it, that Satan is not all-powerful and that he was unable to wreak his uttermost will till I had to do with these as well and even had children by them, whereby the relationship would have become a perfect sink of iniquity. Everything has its limits. The world is finite' (*Der Erwählte*, *GW* VII, p. 258f.; English translation: *The Holy Sinner*, trans. H. Lowe-Porter, London, 1952, pp. 228–9).

11 Adorno is referring to the passage in the chapter 'The Bad Children' where the siblings fear that the howling of the dog Hanegriff will cause them to be discovered: 'And the younker just as he was, half crazed, sprang out of bed for his hunting-knife, seized the dog, and cut his throat, so that with a throat-rattle he stretched his limbs in death; threw the knife on the body, whose blood the sand of the floor drank up; then he turned drunkenly back to the place of another shame. Oh woe for the good and lovely dog! To my mind it was the worst that happened this night, I rather pardon the rest, unlawful as it was. But I suppose it was all of one piece and was not more blameworthy here than there: a spewing of love, murder and passion of the flesh, that may God pity. At least it makes me pitiful' (*GW* VII, p. 36; *The Holy Sinner*, pp. 25–6).

12 In the chapter 'The Duel' (*GW* VII, pp. 134–46; *The Holy Sinner*, pp. 118–27) the war-horse, the 'priceless creature' Sturmi, is described as 'a dappled stallion, of Brabant stock, a blaze on its forehead, with eyes beautiful as the unicorn' (*GW* VII, pp. 144 and 136; *The Holy Sinner*, pp. 126 and 119).

13 The chapter entitled 'The Penance' (*GW* VII, pp. 189–95; *The Holy Sinner*, pp. 167–72).

14 'The penitent spent the winters in timeless winter sleep as small creatures do and during it not even crept out for food, since his physical life was reduced almost to a standstill before it stirred again as the sun's arc increased' (*GW* VII, p. 194; *The Holy Sinner*, p. 171).

15 Arnold Schoenberg had died in Los Angeles on 13 July 1951.

16 The oratorio *Jacob's Ladder* (1917–22) and the opera *Moses and Aaron* (1930–32) both remained unfinished at Schoenberg's death.

17 Hermann Scherchen (1891–1966) premiered the scene of 'The Golden Calf and the Altar', from *Moses and Aaron*, in concert performance on 2 July 1951 in Darmstadt.

18 The 'conservatism' of Schoenberg in Adorno's eyes ('the task of music is to resolve the tensions which it harbours in and through the totality') is expressed in the following passage: 'Every tone which is added to the beginning tone makes the meaning of the tone doubtful. If, for instance, G follows after C, the ear may not be sure whether this expresses C major or G major, or even F major or E minor; and the addition of other tones may or may not clarify this problem. In this manner there is produced a state of unrest, of imbalance, which grows throughout most of the piece, and is enforced further by similar functions of the rhythm. The method by which balance is restored seems to me the real idea of the composition' (Arnold Schoenberg, *Style and Idea*, New York, 1950, p. 49).

19 Thomas Mann did not actually try to thematize the forty-year break in the composition of the work within the text itself. He attempted instead to link the later parts of the work as imperceptibly as possible with the earlier sections.

Gastein, 31 Aug. 51

Dear Dr Adorno, in the greatest of haste, that you might receive this card while you are still here, herewith my deeply felt thanks for your beautiful letter – shame-faced thanks, I should say, since I should have written to you long since about the magnificent 'Minima'. It should not be too long now – we plan to be back home by the beginning of October[1] and urgently hope that we shall still be able to meet up then.

Cordially yours, Thomas Mann

SOURCE: Picture postcard: Weltkurort Badgastein (1083 m.); O: MS; Theodor W. Adorno Archive, Frankfurt am Main.

1 The Manns arrived back in the United States on 7 October.

Zurich, Waldhaus Dolder
18. IX. 51

Dear Dr Adorno,

A quick piece of news – I am giving another lecture in the theatre here on the 24th.[1] On the evening of the 29th we are flying with Swiss Air from Kloten straight to New York, where we shall stay in the Hotel St Regis on 30th and 1st. Since we are expecting to spend a couple of days in Chicago,[2] we shall only arrive in Los Angeles after you have departed – unfortunately enough! Hopefully something will work out in New York.[3] If not – we shall be back over again. Europe does not make me feel particularly dejected.

With all best wishes,

Yours,
Thomas Mann

SOURCE: O: MS; Theodor W. Adorno Archive, Frankfurt am Main.

1 Mann gave a public reading from *Krull* (the two chapters 'Journey and Arrival' and 'Circus') in the Zurich Schauspielhaus on 24 September 1951. His introductory remarks were published in the programme for the Zurich production of Christopher Fry's play *The Lady's not for Burning*

(27 September 1951). See *Tagebücher 1951–1952*, p. 817, and the review of Mann's public reading by Eduard Korrodi in the *Neue Zürcher Zeitung*, 26 September 1951.

2 Thomas Mann's daughter Elisabeth Mann-Borgese (*b*. 1918) and her family were living in Chicago at the time.

3 It proved impossible for Mann and Adorno to meet in New York. Adorno arrived in the city only the day after Mann's departure (see Letter 25, note 4, below).

25   THEODOR W. ADORNO TO THOMAS MANN
     FRANKFURT AM MAIN, 2.1.1952

Frankfurt, 2 January 1952

My dear and esteemed Dr Mann,

I should like to combine my very best wishes for the beginning of 1952 with an expression of utter delight over the two fragments from the new Krull text contained in the last issue of the *Rundschau*.[1] They reveal a beauty and a mastery which far exceed even the most extravagant expectations which I already harboured in this regard, and I am incapable of expressing my thanks in the kind of serene prose that is properly demanded by the recipient of these lines. The manifold layers of meaning, the inner brokenness, the illuminating power of the continuation strike me as quite unique even in your literary output, and the general tone is entirely original and compelling. I am thinking, above all, of the description of the border-crossing,[2] the shameful theft, the conversations with which the little man establishes a rapport with those in authority. Perhaps I may confess to you here that for some years I have constructed a fantasy figure – an imaginary uncle – who talks to his mother, but also to the chief hangman, in a remarkably similar kind of speech that combines trusting friendliness, simple-mindedness and extreme artfulness. In short, I was not only delighted but also slightly conceited to read the work – not least because the shamelessly catatonic insistence with which I kept urging the completion of Krull now finds itself so enchantingly rewarded rather than chastised. Accept my deepest gratitude for this, together with the question of what has become of the original jewel and what you are going to do with it now. This brings me to my principal concern, namely a rumour[3] that you have abandoned Krull in favour of another project. But no, I cannot and will not believe this and would fervently beg you to continue with a creation compared to which Verdi's 'Falstaff' itself will sink to the level of 'The Merry Wives

70

of Windsor'. Please be so kind as to vouchsafe me a few reassuring words in this regard.

We certainly conspired to miss one another very effectively in America. On arriving at St Moritz in New York on our return home I called up St Regis right away only to discover that you had left the previous day – the dates,[4] unless I am mistaken, were the 1st and 2nd of October. It thus seems highly likely that we were actually in Chicago at the same time as you, although we didn't realize it – otherwise I should certainly have exploited the couple of hours we had there to pay you a sudden visit. On the return trip through Chicago I met Kolisch, who is not particularly happy at his university in Wisconsin. But I did learn from him that Schönberg's family is provided for, at least for the coming year.[5]

The hectic days we spent in Los Angeles have now at least made it possible to plan a return trip.[6] We definitely expect to return there in the autumn, and I cannot say how much I am looking forward to seeing you once again.

I have hardly been able to produce much work of my own lately, apart from a fairly extensive plan for a study on Strauss.[7] It is still unclear when I shall have the time to realize the full text. I do not know whether you ever got to see the piece 'Bach Defended against his Devotees'.[8] If not, I could perhaps send it on to you.

I wish you the best of health and further inexhaustible strength for your work.

Heartfelt greetings to you and yours, from Gretel as well,

In true devotion,

Your ancient Devil

SOURCE: O: TS (carbon copy); Theodor W. Adorno Archive, Frankfurt am Main.

1 Thomas Mann, *Bekenntnisse des Hochstaplers Felix Krull: Zwei neue Roman-Fragmente* ['Reise und Ankunft' and 'Cirkus'], published in *Die neue Rundschau*, 62/3 (1951), pp. 1–23; and *Bekenntnisse des Hochstaplers Felix Krull*, GW VII, pp. 385–403 and pp. 451–65; English translation: *Confessions of Felix Krull, Confidence Man: Memoirs Part I*, trans. D. Lindley (London, 1955), pp. 128–46 and pp. 197–211.

2 See *GW* VII, pp. 387–9 and pp. 394–7; *Confessions of Felix Krull*, pp. 138–41.

3 See the following letter.

4 Thomas Mann had arrived in New York on 30 September 1950 and left for Chicago on the following day (see Letter 24). In Chicago he stayed with his daughter Elisabeth Mann-Borgese and her family between 2 and 6 October. Adorno arrived in New York only on 2 October.

71

5 Arnold Schoenberg – who had a daughter, Gertrud (*b.* 1902), and a son, Georg (*b.* 1906), from his first marriage – married Gertrud Kolisch (1898–1967) in 1924. They had a daughter, Nuria (*b.* 1932), who later married the composer Luigi Nono, and two sons, Ronald (*b.* 1937) and Lawrence Adam (*b.* 1941). On reaching retirement in 1944, Schoenberg (who had been an American citizen since 1941) was forced to offer private teaching to support himself. The University of Southern California in Los Angeles, where he had been a member of the academic staff for eight years, paid him a monthly pension of $38.

6 Adorno did return to Los Angeles later in October 1952 and stayed there until August 1953. See Letter 28, note 3, below.

7 A typescript entitled 'ad Strauss' has been preserved among Adorno's literary remains, although it is unclear whether it is related to the plan Adorno mentions here. Since the autumn of 1949 he had been hoping to publish an essay on Richard Strauss for the German newspaper *Merkur* and had corresponded in this regard with the editor, Hans Paeschke. Adorno eventually published an essay on Strauss for the centenary of the composer's birth on 11 July 1964 in *Die neue Rundschau* (pp. 557–87). This essay probably goes back to the plan referred to in the present letter (see GS 16, pp. 565–606).

8 See Adorno, 'Bach gegen seine Liebhaber verteidigt', published first in *Merkur* (5, 1951, pp. 535–46) and later in the collection *Prismen* (GS 10.1, pp. 138–51; English translation: *Prisms*, London, 1969, pp. 133–46).

26   THOMAS MANN TO THEODOR W. ADORNO
     PACIFIC PALISADES, 9.1.1952

THOMAS MANN   1550
                                          SAN REMO DRIVE
                          PACIFIC PALISADES, CALIFORNIA

                                                         9 Jan. 1952

Dear Dr Adorno,
   I am astonished that the enormously busy ordinary professor could find the time for such a long and dearly appreciated new year letter. Many thanks indeed for this – and especially, of course, for your generous words on the chapters from Krull. Why is one prepared to expose such attempts in public if not to receive some encouragement and to counter the awful suspicion, at least momentarily, that perhaps one is simply indulging in a childish play unworthy of a man of my mature years? Otherwise indeed I should never even have thought of publishing these fragments. But these were the same texts I recited in the playhouse in Zurich during the summer, and then Bermann was

asking for something. You can certainly be 'reassured' – insofar as I work on anything at all, I shall be working on *this*. The rumour about my turning to another project is false – and has only arisen, in all likelihood, from scattered remarks in various letters: 'Children, I cannot promise that I shall complete this after all. Perhaps I shall interrupt my work once again – or shall find myself interrupted.' After 'Faustus' I swore that I would never write another long novel, and now I am doing just that – and have simply burdened myself with something which makes demands upon my state of mind and powers of invention that probably go beyond my years. If only I didn't feel this damned inclination to drive anything and everything, even something as foolish as this, into a truly 'Faustian' dimension, to transform it all into a kind of wandering journey through the infinite! I always wanted to pursue this idea and was about to throw myself into it when I started working on my 'German' novel instead.[1] There are also some rather remarkable and amusing aspects to the thing, such as the love affair of the woman who stole the jewels, Mme Houpflé, the factory manager's wife from Strasbourg,[2] an episode which was *not* particularly suitable for recitation in the Zurich playhouse.

What a wonderful form you have chosen, with the 'long aphorism' or the 'short essay' in your 'Minima Moralia'! Have I ever actually thanked you for this book? I believe anything is possible. I hung magnetically upon the book for days, and every day I took it up it proved the most fascinating reading, although it is concentrated fare that can only be enjoyed in small amounts at a time. They say that the twin moon of Sirius, white in colour, is composed of such dense matter that a thimbleful of it would weigh a ton here on earth. That is why it possesses an enormously strong gravitational force-field, just like that which surrounds your book. And then there are the sorrowfully enticing titles that introduce the most breathtaking intellectual insights. Scarcely have I declared 'that is more than enough for today' when along comes another lovely fairy-tale title[3] that draws us headlong into a new adventure.

No, I haven't read 'Bach Defended against his Devotees' and am really very keen to see it – though I am full of serene expectation for the essay on little Richard Strauss which certainly cannot fail to prove highly amusing. The revolutionary as a child of the sun – truly a unique case and entertaining in the best sense. I have always had a considerable amount of time for him, probably because of his great commercial sense. His nonchalance was attractive and with his own enormous talent he was capable of great openness and affection. 'That Mozart! Can he write! It's beyond me!'[4]

It is absurd how we have now managed to miss and pass one another by as we have. And there is some cause for concern that this

73

may *continue* to happen. For if you come to California in the autumn – it is far from clear that we shall be there at the time. We are seriously contemplating the idea of extending our next visit to Europe[5] for a longer period, for a year, perhaps for a couple of years, or however it turns out. The matter must be treated with great caution and discretion, in order to arouse the minimum of publicity, and has hardly begun to be organized as yet. At any rate I trust that we shall sometime meet up again somewhere. All our best wishes to you and to your wife. Yours, Thomas Mann

SOURCE: O: MS; Theodor W. Adorno Archive, Frankfurt am Main. Fp: *Tagebücher 1951–1952*, p. 827f.

1 *Doctor Faustus*.

2 See *Felix Krull*, Part II, chapter 9.

3 Such as 'Wolf as Grandmother' (*GS* 4, pp. 229–33; English translation: *Minima Moralia*, trans. E. F. N. Jephcott, London, 1974, pp. 203–6).

4 It has not been possible to identify a published source of this remark, which may have been reported from a private conversation.

5 Thomas and Katia Mann travelled to Switzerland, via Chicago and New York, on 24 June 1952. After recuperating for a short time in Kandersteg, they made further trips to Lugano, Zurich, Munich, Salzburg, St Wolfgang, Bad Gastein, Frankfurt am Main and Vienna. The Manns never returned to the United States and on 24 December 1952 they moved into Haus Erlenbach, Glärnichstrasse 12, in Zurich.

27   THOMAS MANN TO THEODOR W. ADORNO
     PACIFIC PALISADES, 12.2.1952

THOMAS MANN   1550
                                              SAN REMO DRIVE
                              PACIFIC PALISADES, CALIFORNIA

                                                   12 Feb. 52

Dear Dr Adorno,
  You have regaled me with a veritable wealth of material.[1] Many thanks for this. No one has ever written better and more perceptively on the subject of 'Unrat',[2] and I am in some position to judge here. I am less confident in expressing an opinion on Bach, but I have the strong impression that here too you have given powerful expression to what it is right and necessary to say – I still have to read 'Cultural Criticism and

Society',[3] when I am less tired that is. For to read your work, one should certainly not be tired.

Incidentally I myself despatched a very sharp letter to Rowohlt about the 'title' issue,[4] and have received a rather sheepish and apologetic reply.

I am pushing on as vigorously as my strength permits with the 'Confessions' – the pan-erotic amorality of which is not even remotely suggested by the published fragments – and am also putting together a collection of essays entitled 'Things Old and New – Shorter Writings from Five Decades'.[5] This demands a lot of effort, but then it is also rather enjoyable to gather one's gleanings into the barn.

May everything go well for your part. More power to you![6]

Yours,
Thomas Mann

SOURCE: O: MS with printed letterhead; Theodor W. Adorno Archive, Frankfurt am Main. Pp: *Tagebücher 1951–1952*, p. 584, and *DüD*, p. 489.

1 It is not known whether Adorno also sent an accompanying letter with the essays in question.

2 The Rowohlt publishing house had recently brought out the novel *Professor Unrat* (1905) by Heinrich Mann (1871–1950) in a paperback edition under the title *The Blue Angel* (that of the film version of the story from 1932). The publishers hoped to encourage sales of the new edition by substituting the film title for the original one. Adorno had written a piece demanding restoration of the author's title, since the novel itself was incompatible with the conformist approach typified by the film: 'If the verdict dictated by sales had not unquestioningly been accepted as the decisive consideration here, the damaged work could properly be honoured once again by eliminating this symbol of accommodation, the false title, and restoring the original one' (see Adorno, 'Warum nicht "Prof. Unrat"? Zu einem geänderten Titel', *Die neue Zeitung*, 25 January 1952, p. 4; *GS* 11, pp. 654–7, passage quoted on p. 657). Rowohlt responded evasively in a letter of 28 January, suggesting that the author himself had sanctioned the change of title and that the East Berlin publisher Aufbau Verlag bore ultimate responsibility in the matter. Adorno replied in an article entitled 'Unrat and Angel', published in *Die neue Zeitung* on 18 February (p. 4), which concluded with the following words: 'Once it was left to potentates and statesmen to say "I never wished it so" when they had instigated a war. Today every film scriptwriter, every block leader, says the same without even having to lie about it. Everyone makes himself into an idiot. Irresponsibility is no longer a privilege. The ruin is total' (see *GS* 11, pp. 658–60).

3 See Theodor W. Adorno, 'Kulturkritik und Gesellschaft', in *Soziologische Forschung in unserer Zeit: Ein Sammelwerk Leopold von Wiese zum 75*

Geburtstag, ed. Karl Gustav Specht (Cologne and Opladen, 1951), pp. 228–40; *GS* 10.1, pp. 11–30; English translation: *Prisms*, London, 1969, pp. 17–34.

4 A transcript of Thomas Mann's letter to Rowohlt from Bad Gastein (4 September 1951) has survived:

> Dear Herr Rowohlt,
> I observe that you have announced a reissue, in your economy series, of Heinrich Mann's novel '*Professor Unrat*' under the title 'The Blue Angel'. Perhaps you would be so kind as to inform me by what right you intend to do so and, in particular, who has authorized you to substitute the title in question. I believe I can assume that my departed brother himself would never have permitted his book to be published under the name of the film.
>
> The situation with regard to the literary remains of my brother is an extremely complex one. Heinrich Mann died without leaving a will and, in accordance with American practice, the whole of his estate, including current publishing rights and royalties, has been appropriated, for the foreseeable future, by the 'Public Administrator' in California. The 'Administrator' is preparing to sell my brother's American estate and will do everything possible to collect any payments still due to the estate (in all the Western European countries). My brother's daughter, Frau Askenazy, would hardly therefore have the right to offer you a licensed edition of the work. Whatever the exact situation in this regard, I should be grateful to receive any further information from you concerning your plans in relation to 'Professor Unrat'. Above all, however, I would repeat my belief that I am acting in the name of my departed brother in regarding the publication of his book under the title 'The Blue Angel' as unacceptable in any case, irrespective of the manner in which you may have acquired the rights to do so.
>
> With sincere and devoted regards, [Thomas Mann]

The publishing house replied on 10 September, indicating that they had forwarded a copy of Mann's letter to the Berlin publisher Aufbau Verlag, which had originally agreed the rights for a licensed edition with Rowohlt Verlag. Rowohlt received clarification from Aufbau Verlag concerning their view of the matter on 14 September, and this was immediately passed on to Thomas Mann. Heinrich Maria Ledig-Rowohlt then wrote to Thomas Mann, indicating Rowohlt's view that Erich Wendt, the director of Aufbau Verlag, had correctly stated the legal position as far as the author's and the publisher's rights were concerned. Ledig-Rowohlt also pointed out that Heinrich Mann's *Professor Unrat* had already appeared under the new title in 1947 in the first post-war edition of the work (published by A. Weichert in Berlin) and that, according to the foreword of this edition, the change of title had in fact been expressly sanctioned by Heinrich Mann. 'This information has thankfully relieved my father's conscience in this matter, since he was very strongly opposed to adopting the title of the film in the first place. It was only the fact that a new edition of the book had already appeared under this title, and the fact that our own economically priced edition was aimed at reaching a broader circle of readers, which eventually overcame the original reservations which he had often passionately expressed to us here before. We should also point out that our edition explicitly indicates that the work was first published in 1905 under the title "Professor Unrat", as well as the fact that the "introduction" to our little volume also clarifies these matters in greater detail in the context of Heinrich Mann's work as a whole' (undated letter to Thomas Mann, transcript preserved in the collection of Otto Mayer, Düsseldorf).

5 This material appeared in the 'Stockholmer Gesamtausgabe' (Frankfurt am Main, 1953) of Thomas Mann's works. The relevant volume includes eighty-three pieces of one kind or another, arranged under the following rubrics: 'Essays', 'Speeches', 'Introductions and Literary Reviews', 'Politics', 'Autobiography', 'Miscellanies' and 'Letters'.

6 The words 'More power to you!' are in English in the original text.

28 THEODOR W. ADORNO TO THOMAS MANN
     FRANKFURT AM MAIN, 13.4.1952

Frankfurt/Main 13 April 1952
123 Kettenhofweg

My dear and esteemed Dr Mann,
    If it is only now that I feel able to respond to your extremely informative lines from February last, this is because your letter provoked in me a certain anxiety that is difficult to formulate in words and which for that very reason has hindered me from writing to you earlier. Delighted though I was to hear about the progress of your work on 'Krull' and the shift of emphasis which has clearly affected your original conception, I could hardly help but sense an undertone of sadness in your words. Insofar as this cannot be explained simply by the enormous concentration that such work requires, something which particularly in your own case is always directly reflected in your physical constitution itself, it is surely your thoughts concerning the current course of the world which are largely responsible for this. I should certainly not wish to cast matters in a fairer light than they deserve, and for my own part I believe I can truly say that, even in so-called better times, whether those of my own youth or those of the Roosevelt period,[1] I have never really placed any trust in the prevailing circumstances or conditions – which is perhaps why sudden manifestations of disaster in so many different contexts have rarely proved a cause of much surprise to me. And even today the situation appears largely the same. But on the other hand I believe that we have nonetheless been granted a certain breathing space in this respect; that you should certainly not lose heart about realizing the fundamental

conception of your current work; that there is indeed a chance that the ultimate catastrophe may be averted in our own lifetime. It would be difficult to explain here the reasons which encourage me in this view, but I have weighed them so seriously that I have chosen to remain here, almost on the Russian border as it were, even in times of the most urgent clamour. And the internal situation on your own side of the world, as I was able to gather, even from the television, while I was over there during the autumn, is still not one of drastic threat. Among the demands that face our historical capacity to react and respond to events today, the necessity for differentiating even in matters of the negative is certainly not the least. The fact that people were not sufficiently capable of doing so in Germany before, that they could not differentiate between Brüning[2] and Hitler, was itself partly responsible for the disaster which eventually ensued. And I would appeal to this kind of shaming reflection here.

Of course I also have highly selfish reasons for thinking along these lines. In the autumn we shall definitely both be back over for a fairly long period of time[3] (though I would ask that you keep this to yourself, since it would really set tongues wagging here in Germany if the news should get out prematurely). I have to come back for a while if only to secure continued citizenship. I should be literally inconsolable if I were to miss you on this occasion too and to discover you had returned to Switzerland in the meantime. But I also know how to rationalize my selfishness in these matters. It is not simply that my political prognoses have been abundantly confirmed in the past. For I have also learned that in a fundamental sense there is no returning, that Europe has become as foreign as a foreign country itself, and, more importantly, that it is now urgently limping after other lines of development, albeit in an often rather clumsy and inefficient fashion. To put it bluntly, you would certainly encounter just as many, and probably more, difficulties over here, and I feel the most important thing is that you manage to preserve those conditions under which you are best able, as you put it, to gather your gleanings into the barn. But one of the most crucial things in this respect, it seems to me, is surely to spare yourself the chthonic upheaval of yet another change of residence. Perhaps this is all rather foolish advice, and really just an expression of selfishness on my part, but I cannot resist the impulse to utter it nonetheless.

I have little new to report about my own circumstances. I have a lot of work to do, and since I am already explicitly thinking of packing up my bags, this only makes it all the more difficult to discharge my duties rather than less. But I still hope, in the not too distant future, to be able to send you something properly trimmed and finished. A couple of weeks ago my mother died in New York at the age of eighty-seven.[4] And just because our last meeting was actually so sad – I hardly recognized her any more than she recognized herself – the final parting has affected me very deeply. With a loved one we are tempted to regard even the decline that accompanies extreme old age as a merely temporary state, and we can only hope that we are ultimately right to do so.

A public reading from the writings of Bruno Frank, under the aegis of his wife,[5] took place here a couple of days ago, and I recalled what you once told me about the misunderstanding that arose when the poor fellow was bold enough to try and learn from you.

I learned from Stuckenschmidt,[6] who gave a lecture here recently, that you were eventually reconciled with Schönberg after all.[7] It is not a matter of mere curiosity if I could ask you to let me know sometime whether this is indeed the case. Only, of course, if you have nothing better to do one day and you really feel inclined to do so. For I can hardly bear the thought of holding you back from your own work even for a second.

We are now off to Baden-Baden for ten days, and even if the Hotel Stefanie is inaccessible because of the occupation, I can still imagine that your Krull would certainly have felt at home there.

Best wishes to you and yours, from Gretel too,

Yours devotedly,

As always

Teddie Adorno

SOURCE: O: TS with handwritten corrections; Thomas Mann Archive, Zurich.

1 Franklin Delano Roosevelt (1882–1945), the thirty-second president of the United States, who occupied the office between 1933 and 1945. Mann had given a speech in support of Roosevelt's election campaign on 29 October 1944 and delivered a memorial address for Roosevelt on 15 April 1945. (See 'Rede für Franklin D. Roosevelt im Wahlkampf 1944', in *Reden und Aufsätze* III, *GW* XI, pp. 979–83, and 'Franklin Roosevelt', in *Reden und Aufsätze* IV, *GW* XII, pp. 941–4.)

2 Heinrich Brüning (1885–1970), German politician of the centre and member of the Reichstag from 1924. He was the German chancellor from 1930 until 1932, when he was dismissed by General von Hindenburg. In order to avoid arrest by the National Socialists Brüning emigrated in 1934 to the United States, where he subsequently taught at Harvard University.

3 Adorno returned to the United States between October 1952 and August 1953 in his capacity as research director of the Hacker Foundation in Beverly Hills (*GS* 10.2, p. 732). During this period he composed the study on the astrology column of the *Los Angeles Times*, 'The Stars Down to Earth' (*GS* 9.2,

pp. 7–120), which also formed the basis for his German essay 'Aberglaube aus zweiter Hand' [Superstition Second Hand] (*GS* 8, pp. 147–76), and the study 'How to Look at Television', which appeared in 1954 in the *Hollywood Quarterly of Film, Radio and Television* (vol. 8, pp. 214–35), and contributed materials to the German essay 'Fernsehen und Ideologie' [Television and Ideology] (*GS* 10.2, pp. 518–32). Adorno would forfeit his American citizenship if he were absent from the country for more than three years.

4 Maria Wiesengrund had died on 23 February 1952.

5 The poet and writer Bruno Frank (1887–1945) lived and worked as an independent writer in Munich until 1933. He emigrated to Switzerland that year and subsequently moved to London. In 1937 he left for the United States and settled in California in the vicinity of the Manns. The writer was known principally for his *Politische Novelle* (1928), his historical novel *Cervantes* (1934) and his 'exile novel' *Der Reisepass* (1937). Nothing further is known about the reading that took place in the presence of Liesl Frank (1903–1978).

6 The composer, writer and music critic Hans Heinz Stuckenschmidt (1901–1988) was appointed professor for the history of music at the Technical University in Berlin in 1949. He published his major study *Arnold Schönberg* in 1952. Nothing further is known about the specific lecture to which Adorno refers here.

7 See the following letter, as well as Letter 13, note 1, and Letter 16, notes 4, 5 and 6.

29 THOMAS MANN TO THEODOR W. ADORNO
    PACIFIC PALISADES, 19–21.4.1952

THOMAS MANN   1550
                                               SAN REMO DRIVE
                                  PACIFIC PALISADES, CALIFORNIA

                                                     19 April 1952

Dear Dr Adorno,
    I must thank you right away for your tactful and sensitive letter. You have indeed detected something that I was myself quite unconscious of expressing in my lines to you. My life has really entered upon a kind of crisis, and pre-eminently a crisis in my work. These Krull memoirs have created in me a degree of anxious concern that is out of all proportion to the extent of their possible merit. A stylized novel of this kind is a *mer à boire*, and I should never have burdened myself with such an undertaking in the first place. There is simply no way, with respect either to its subject matter or to its artistic ambitions, that the task is properly *de mon âge*. Pan-eroticism and diamond thievery – should one

80

really be wasting all the energies of one's latter years upon jests like this? And such tiring and difficult jests![1] Since I started working on the thing again – though without definitely committing myself to finishing the task – all sorts of remarkable new ideas have taken shape; but they lack the straightforward enjoyment of the parts composed more than forty years ago. I shall continue working on it, but I am often strongly tempted to abandon the thing and just leave it as an expanded fragment. But this doesn't entirely appeal to me either for I am a doer and a finisher, and have never been one simply to 'leave things at that'. In short, it is quite true that I am feeling rather downcast – and the current world situation is not without an effect in this regard, as you rightly surmise. I do not actually believe that there will be outright war either. Europe does not want it, Russia surely does not want it at any price, and simply on our own 'we' cannot want it either without making ourselves appear morally quite impossible. But the very rage that war is indeed unthinkable only means that the mood will become ever more unpleasant and the air ever more difficult to breathe over here. The way things are developing is already clear. And we have rather gone beyond Brüning. For under Brüning we were not yet confronted, for example, by thousands of people deprived of employment as a result of their non-conformist views. The hatred, the taste for persecution, the terrorizing of attitudes and opinions, the enforced silence, the nameless hypocrisy, mendacity and self-righteousness, the hopeless weakness and cowed reticence of those who know better, the fact alone that someone like McCarthy cannot be neutralized, that he can rely on ever-increasing financial support, that his shady methods and techniques have effectively become established practice – all this only encourages the thought of taking flight yet again. But of taking flight to where, you will naturally ask. And you are right, there is nowhere to escape these things. Europe has become a wretched colony. But, remarkably enough, the more miserable the condition of Europe actually becomes, the more I feel myself to be a European and, as I have already said, I am still drawn back to the earth 'from which I was taken'. Returning to Germany is out of the question, that would be too uncanny – even though the simplest thing would be to build a new and smaller house on the beautiful land we own on the Isar (the old ruin has been demolished) and I could once again go walking to the Aumeister. But this would all be just too ghostly now. I do love Switzerland, I have trust in this well-governed country that is neutral territory after all, and I have been corresponding with people in Bern[2] who have displayed a really warm and welcoming attitude towards us. On the other hand, you are quite right in thinking it is rather late in the day to contemplate such a dramatic change of existence, to consider settling elsewhere all over again. The havoc involved is already making me anxious, and I would certainly

81

think the matter over even *longer* were it not for Erika – who is simply losing heart through the total lack of any real activity here. So the whole situation is rather like that of the novel itself – extremely distressing. And everything is taking its time too: the house cannot easily be sold at once and we shall have to wait a while for the right opportunity. This year we shall be taking the usual trip to Europe[3] and returning here in the autumn – so it seems, and thus we look forward to seeing you then.

The business with Schönberg fell out as follows.[4] He had published yet another insipid piece of his own in an English journal (the editor described it as a 'character document'). I wrote to him saying that before I finally succumbed to his repeated assaults he should at least allow me to publish the earlier letter in which he had expressed complete satisfaction over my willingness to comply with his wishes in this matter. He responded that I had now won him over and reconciled him to me, that we should bury the hatchet and be good friends henceforth. He indicated that he did not really wish to advertise our reconciliation publicly since it might seem to betray those who had already supported his cause in the dispute. But he suggested we should give public expression to our peace settlement on some suitable occasion like an eightieth birthday celebration. An excellent idea, I responded, and indicated that I had always been determined not to reciprocate his hostility, as he had surely already noticed from my earlier reply in the S.R.L.[5] And that is where the matter rested. I never saw him again, and unfortunately he did not reach his eightieth birthday after all.

All best wishes to you and your dear wife from me and mine,

Yours,

Thomas Mann

Do forgive the script.[6] I think you will be able to read it and it proves quicker for me to write this way.

SOURCE: O: MS with printed letterhead; Theodor W. Adorno Archive, Frankfurt am Main. Pp: Thomas Mann, *Tagebücher 1951–1952*, p. 628ff.

1 An allusion to Goethe's remarks on his Faust drama in a letter to Wilhelm von Humboldt of 17 March 1832: 'It would naturally be an infinite joy to me if during my lifetime, too, I could dedicate these serious jests to my valued friends everywhere. I have always been grateful for their interest and should like to hear their response' (*Goethes Werke*, Vol. 49: *Goethes Briefe* (Weimar, 1909; repr. Munich, 1987), p. 283).

2 At the end of 1951 Thomas Mann had resumed his correspondence with Ernst Nobs (1886–1957), a deputy of the Swiss Federal Parliament, whom he had first met at a Goethe commemoration in Zurich in June 1949. Mann was considering the idea of settling in Tessin and wrote to Nobs, who had taken over

at the Department of Finance and Customs in 1951, to enquire about conditions of entry and residence and associated tax issues. On 12 September 1951 Mann noted in his diary: 'Have received detailed response from Deputy Nobs about residence qualifications, tax matters etc. The relevant information is satisfactory. Delighted by the remark: "The canton of Tessin, like Switzerland itself, will count itself honoured if you decide to settle here"' (*Tagebücher 1951–1952*, p. 146). Mann responded to Nobs's letter, which has not survived, on the same day: 'We have now taken our first steps towards selling the house that we built here eleven years ago so that we can acquire a particular currently available property near Lugano, which Emil Oprecht first drew to our attention, and which will require very little modification for our needs. We had thought of the canton of Tessin on account of the climate, for we have already been spoilt by the Californian light. But also, and especially, because my old friend Hermann Hesse is living there too. Your letter has fully set my mind at rest about the conditions of residence, and the tax situation is also a lot clearer to me now' (copy from the Thomas Mann Archive). Double taxation of income was forbidden as a consequence of an agreement between Switzerland and the United States that was signed on 24 May 1951. Ernst Nobs's reply of 26 December, preserved in the Mann Archive, assured Mann that he could count on the full support of the Swiss authorities in these matters: 'I have taken it upon myself to send a copy [of Mann's letter] to our federal president, who heads the department dealing with foreign residents, and likewise to Director Amstutz at the Central Tax Office, which will always be ready to assist with any information concerning double taxation arrangements with the United States.'

3 See Letter 26, note 6.

4 See Letter 16, notes 4, 5 and 6.

5 Mann is referring to the *Saturday Review of Literature*. See the note to Letter 13.

6 The letter is written in classical German script.

30 THEODOR W. ADORNO TO THOMAS MANN
FRANKFURT AM MAIN, 28.4.1952

Frankfurt, 28 April 1952

My dear and esteemed Dr Mann,

May I reply at once to your letter of 19 April by which I was most deeply moved? You must not, for God's sake, allow yourself to become depressed about the difficulties you are encountering in connection with 'Krull'. These difficulties are precisely a testimony to the fecundity of your own conception of the work. For a work of art only properly comes to grips with its material in the moment when it engages with the internal contradictions of the latter, and these contradictions then translate

83

themselves inevitably into the problem of artistic form itself. If we fail to encounter such difficulties, then – at least in the sense of the sole and highest criterion – it is surely not worth starting at all. If your artistic conception now seems remote from the wonderful things which you composed forty years ago, I certainly cannot regard this as any real cause for anxiety on your part. For something similar has happened with all great conceptions that have accompanied their creators over the career of a lifetime, and such conceptions are all marked, if viewed from the perspective of a classicist aesthetic, by a certain fragmentariness. But it is precisely this fragmentary dimension that leads us into the essence of epic form itself, which is intrinsically concerned with broad and extensive themes and can in principle never be 'finished' in quite the same way as dramatic or symphonic art can be. And indeed if form itself, in the highest kind of narrative literature, assumes a dynamic and protean character, if such works thereby transcend their own purely immanent form, this strikes me as a telling sign that the achieved artistic representation is only obeying the internally governed movement of the matter in question. For is it really any different, if I may here extend the concept of epic art far beyond the literal conception of the genre, with 'The Master',[1] with 'Faust', with 'The Ring'? In the last case there is not only the famous break in the composition of 'Siegfried',[2] but the fact that the language and artistic procedures actually change from work to work, indeed from act to act, throughout the cycle. And if the whole of 'The Ring' also involves, among other things, a certain demythologizing process, from the Valhalla of 'Rheingold' through to the Hall of the Gibichungs where Alberich finally appears simply as a dream image, then this progressive humanization of the action also communicates itself to the ever less distanced and ever more passionate character of the inner musical treatment. And as far as 'Faust' is concerned – where I must confess that I have never really understood the old scholarly controversy about 'the wager' – it always struck me as far more illuminating and also more profound that the wager is *forgotten* in the rest of the action and subsequently ignored by the reflective author himself. And this is how open-ended and fragmentary life forgets what actually set it moving in the first place, only to recall it once again at the final moment like something glimpsed from afar. (For Alberich too has only three words to sing at the close of the 'Twilight of the Gods'.[3]) This is naturally not the sort of thing that can be planned in advance. On the contrary – if it were so planned, it would turn out to be impossible. But if something eventually turns out to be right, and if in the end your own 'Krull' has as little to do with the playful images of its beginning as Siegfried's death has to do with the initial sporting of the Rhinemaidens, that is certainly no misfortune. It merely shows that such an artistic conception harbours incomparably greater powers and energies within itself than it could possibly dare to imagine at the start. Remain true, therefore, to the thought of 'completion' and content yourself with *that* fragmentary moment that itself lies within the matter in question and that will only fully shine forth once the whole work is concluded.

And what is more, one really should not allow oneself to be terrorized by the concept of stylistic unity. Here Schönberg was quite right, for all his lack of conceptual reflection, in polemically opposing the artistic idea to the so-called will to style.[4] This has become particularly clear to me in connection with the correspondence between Strauss and Hofmannsthal,[5] which has now been published *in extenso*, albeit with a number of unforgivable omissions, and a copy of which I am sure you will already possess. This is an uncommonly instructive document. It is certainly not the case that either of them, of whom incidentally, on closer inspection, Strauss surprisingly makes a rather better impression, was concerned simply with success or unwilling to expend serious thought upon their operas. It is merely that they reflected upon their work from the top down, as it were, from the perspective of style, of overcoming the Wagnerian moment, of reconciling the German and Italian traditions, of attaining a kind of Nietzschean serenity. And that is why everything has an attenuated and rather experimental character about it. If they had only lavished the same intensity and conscientiousness of reflection upon the inner musical treatment and the developing musical language as they did upon the style and overall dramaturgy of the works, then the second half of Strauss's oeuvre would not have simply represented the film version of the first. The way in which you set about your work is entirely different in this respect. Instead of sampling one approach after another you immerse yourself with an unparalleled trust and capacity for creative self-regeneration in the task at hand, in the language of words which is the sole material of literature; you are not concerned with producing types or genres of works, but compose your work differently, measure by measure, precisely as you proceed. And then you find that the particular modification of specific genres falls to you in and of itself like a gift. I can hardly express the boundless trust and confidence with which I await the completion of 'Krull'. Is the transformed character of the work, which you acknowledge with such trepidation, not itself a reflection of the chthonic changes which have affected existence as such, and thus also the *a priori* form of great art, over the last forty years?

See how, in trying to appease you and, contrary to other kinds of appeasement, to shield you from defeatism, I have now held forth at length like a proper professor of aesthetics – and perhaps you will smile over someone who spouts such foolish-clever talk six thousand miles away from the task in hand just because this is so easy to do, just because he looks upon these questions concerning the appropriate

85

artistic form of the work entirely from the outside, instead of actually having to struggle with them line for line himself. But if you credit me with enough imagination to understand your own predicament, I think that you will eventually find a kernel of truth in what I have tried to say. I should merely like to make a modest contribution to something that will surely transpire anyway: the transformation of difficulty and resistance into true productive energy.

I am very relieved that you have at least postponed your plans for moving again in a way that means we may still have an opportunity for discussing things before you come to a definitive decision on the matter. I certainly do not dispute the complicated and involved character of the whole question. Basically I believe that in every possible sense the difference between Europe and America today is indeed infinitely *smaller* than it actually appears from the perspective of our own desires and aspirations. The question therefore really acquires an aspect of rationality and thoughtful planning that makes it susceptible to intelligent discussion.

I should also just like to mention the enormous pleasure with which I read an essay by Golo in the journal 'Monat'[6] where he effectively clips the claims of our dear Reichenbach. What kind of philosophy is this that can conflate the delusive self-confidence of the mathematics teacher with truth, the methods of the natural sciences with the theory of knowledge!

Please do keep me informed about your future plans, including those for another European trip.

The best of greetings to your family from both of us, and particularly to Erika,

Most devotedly yours,

Teddie Adorno

A writer whom I have not come across before, one Jean Boyer, has recently published an extensive study 'A propos du rôle de la musique dans le "Doktor Faustus" de Thomas Mann' in the 'Annales' of the Faculté des Lettres de Toulouse.[7]

SOURCE: O: TS with handwritten corrections; Thomas Mann Archive, Zurich.

1 Adorno is alluding to Goethe's novel *Wilhelm Meister*.

2 Wagner had set aside his work on the second act of *Siegfried* in 1857. He finally completed the score in 1871.

3 Adorno is thinking of the final words of Hagen – not Alberich, as he mistakenly writes here – at the very end of the third act of *Twilight of the Gods*: 'Zurück vom Ring!' [Away from the Ring!].

4 See Arnold Schoenberg, 'New Music, Outmoded Music, Style and Idea', in his book *Style and Idea* (New York, 1950), pp. 37–51.

5 See Richard Strauss and Hugo Hofmannsthal, *Briefwechsel*, ed. Franz Strauss and Alice Strauss, rev. Willi Schuh (Zurich, 1952). The Thomas Mann Library in Zurich holds a copy of the book with a personal dedication from Willi Schuh from April 1952.

6 See Golo Mann, 'Wissenschaft statt Philosophie' [Science instead of Philosophy], *Der Monat* 4 (1952), pp. 420–4. The essay is essentially a critical review of *The Rise of Scientific Philosophy*, the last book by Hans Reichenbach (1891–1953). Reichenbach was forced by the National Socialists to abandon his chair in Berlin in 1933. He taught in Istanbul from 1933 to 1938 before settling in the United States, where he taught at the University of California until his death in 1953.

7 See Jean Boyer, 'A propos du rôle de la musique dans le "Doktor Faustus" ', *Annales publiées par la Faculté des Lettres de Toulouse*, December 1951, pp. 119–43. Jean Boyer (1888–1950) was a Germanist and musicologist who taught in Toulouse. The copy of the essay, which the author personally sent to Mann, is preserved in the Thomas Mann Archive.

31   THEODOR W. ADORNO TO THOMAS MANN
     FRANKFURT AM MAIN, 26.9.1952

T. W. Adorno   26 Sept. 1952

Dr Thomas Mann
Waldhaus Dolder
Zurich, Switzerland

My dear and esteemed Dr Mann,
    Yesterday I learned from the theatre people with whom I spent the evening after an extraordinarily fine performance of Verdi's 'Otello' that you will be in Frankfurt at the beginning of November.[1] I am quite disconsolate about this since I am departing for Los Angeles on 15 October because of citizenship formalities and also various academic commitments. I shall spend a couple of days in Paris before going to New York, and then on to Santa Monica at the beginning of November, where we have succeeded in reclaiming the last apartment we used to have there.
    I cannot bear the thought that we shall miss one another yet again – though you must forgive this crude confession on my part. On the other hand, as you can easily imagine, I am so tied up with the affairs of the institute in these last few weeks that I cannot leave Frankfurt at

the moment. I am writing to you now in the desperate hope that your own travels may take you through Paris between 15 and 21 October, or might at least be encouraged to pass by that way – if you do not regard this as a shameless suggestion. I have no real material excuse for this apart from my burning desire to see you. Please be so kind as to write me a few lines in this connection.

The little Wagner book came out a few days ago,[2] though I have taken the opportunity of fundamentally revising chapters III, VII and VIII. Perhaps you will not find it too tedious to look through the text once again.

Dearest and fairest wishes to you both, from Gretel too

Most devotedly yours,

[Teddie Adorno]

SOURCE: O: TS (carbon copy); Theodor W. Adorno Archive, Frankfurt am Main.

1 See the following letter.

2 See Letter 2, note 2.

32 THOMAS MANN TO THEODOR W. ADORNO
   ZURICH, 30.9.1952

Zurich, 30 Sept. 52

Dear Dr Adorno,

This is all very distressing. You are correctly informed: I am coming to Frankfurt on 8 November, in order to give a speech in the Schauspielhaus on the afternoon of the 9th to inaugurate the Gerhart Hauptmann Theatre Festival Week.[1] I am working on my speech at the moment, which is quite a trial,[2] but for a variety of reasons I have been unable to evade this task. And now I learn you will not be there. This is fate. Such an unfriendly turn of events. I should have left with greater enthusiasm if the prospect of our meeting had beckoned. But now it beckons only feebly from afar. For while you are going back, we shall almost certainly *not* return, but will now be remaining over here. And I shall not be conveyed to Paris in October,[3] but only to Munich and Vienna,[4] – no, I am wrong, the trip to Vienna is late November, and I shall be in Munich only between 17 and 19 October. But you are leaving on the 15th – would it be possible for you to break your journey to Paris and stop off in Zurich on the 16th? A wholly impractical idea, I imagine, but I don't know what else to suggest. I must simply console myself with the thought that, even if we have no intention of returning to California, you will come back to Europe again (?) in my own lifetime.

And now your book on Wagner has appeared! Surely you will send me a copy? I shall devour it like the one in the Book of Revelation who consumes a book which tastes 'as sweet as honey'.[5]

All best wishes to you and your wife,

Yours,

Thomas Mann

SOURCE: O: MS; Theodor W. Adorno Archive, Frankfurt am Main. Pp: *DüD*, p. 533.

1 Thomas Mann stayed in Frankfurt from 8 to 11 November. His speech 'Gerhart Hauptmann' was first published as volume 52 in the series 'Das kleine Buch' (Gütersloh, 1953). See Thomas Mann, *Reden und Aufsätze* I, *GW* IX, pp. 804–15. On 10 November Mann gave a public reading of the 'Cuckoo' chapter from *Felix Krull* in the Great Hall of Frankfurt University. Max Horkheimer, as rector of the university, delivered the welcome address (which was largely written by Adorno). See Max Horkheimer, *Gesammelte Schriften*, vol. 13, pp. 255–8, and Adorno, *GS* 20.2, pp. 467–72.

2 The relationship between Thomas Mann and Gerhart Hauptmann (1862–1946) was always a difficult one – 'something resembling friendship', as Mann himself described it in 1949. Mann was frequently requested to speak in honour of Hauptmann, even, as in this case, after the writer's death.

3 Mann is alluding to Felix Krull's journey to Paris in part II, chapter 7, of the novel. Questioned by the conductor on the train, Krull says 'That is where I am being conveyed' (*GW* VII, p. 387).

4 Mann travelled to Munich on 17 October. On 19 October he gave another reading of the 'Cuckoo' chapter from *Felix Krull*. Mann was in Vienna from 17 till 26 November, and on 18 November he gave a talk on 'The Artist and Society' in the Mozart Hall of the Vienna Concert House. He had broadcast the same talk in English on the BBC in May 1952.

5 Revelation 10: 9–10. The writer is commanded to eat the book by the Angel. In his copy of the Bible, Mann had marked the following passage: 'Und er sprach zu mir: Nimm hin und verschling's, und es wird dich im Bauch grimmen; aber in deinem Munde wird's süss sein wie Honig. Und ich nahm das Büchlein von der Hand des Engels und verschlang's; und es war süss in meinem Munde wie Honig, und da ich's gegessen hatte, grimmte mich's im Bauch' (*Die Heiligen Schriften des Alten und Neuen Bundes deutsch von Martin Luther*, Munich and Leipzig [1910], vol. 4, p. 470). In the King James version the passage reads as follows: 'And he said unto me, Take it, and eat it up; and it shall make thy belly bitter, but it shall be in thy mouth sweet as honey. / And I took the little book out of the angel's hand, and ate it up; and it was in my mouth sweet as honey: and as soon as I had eaten it, my belly was bitter.'

Theodor W. Adorno

6 October 1952

My dear and esteemed Dr Mann,

I had imagined as much – we shall miss one another yet again. You may believe me when I say that I certainly considered paying you a sudden visit in Zurich. Otherwise my own attempt to lure you to Paris would have been entirely presumptuous, however much Paris recommends itself for other reasons as the right place for such a rendezvous. But I simply cannot get away from here early enough to fit in a detour via Zurich. I do not have to tell you how saddened I am as a result. If only I had suspected you were in Munich.[1] But I learned this after you had already left. I can now only hope that I shall be back in Europe very soon and will be able to see you then. It is very likely I shall be back unless the Passport Division makes things really difficult. For the research plans in Los Angeles and in our own institute here are intimately connected with one another, and some kind of shuttle service between here and there will certainly be required for purely material reasons anyway. As far as this otherwise rather disagreeable prospect is concerned, the possibility of seeing you once again at last is the only ray of light.

I was very saddened to hear about the death of Alfred Neumann.[2] I know how much his friendship meant to you and I have fond memories of him myself. I can easily imagine, especially in the almost unbearably oppressive objective circumstances of the present, how much this loss among those closest to you will inevitably affect you – and I feel for you at this time.

It is a great pity that I cannot be here on the days you are planning to spend in Frankfurt. Horkheimer, who, as you probably know, has now been elected rector for the second time,[3] is looking forward enormously to your visit and would like you to get in touch the moment you arrive; there are so many things to discuss. His private address: Westendstrasse 79, and his private telephone number: 72540. And perhaps you would also enjoy taking a look at the institute, which we have literally stamped forth out of the ground here.

Would there be any chance of obtaining a copy of your speech on art and society[4] in the near future? I shall naturally consume it with double relish. I hope the book on Wagner is already in your hands. I am very eager to hear your judgement on this material – which at once goes so far back and yet is still so close that it all appears to me like a blurred dream.

Once I am back over there, I hope to be able to work again on something philosophical at last and complete a really long-standing project.[5]

I should be very grateful if I could hear a word or two from you before I leave, especially with regard to 'Krull', about which people have been murmuring wonderful things. I shall be here until the 15th, and then at the Hotel Régina in Paris until the 21st.

Fairest greetings from Gretel,

Yours devotedly,

[Teddie Adorno]

SOURCE: O: TS (carbon copy); Theodor W. Adorno Archive, Frankfurt am Main.

1 Thomas Mann had been in Munich between 9 and 11 August. His talk on 'The Artist and Society' was broadcast by South German Radio.

2 The writer and dramatist Alfred Neumann (1895–1952) had died in Lugano in the night of 2–3 October 1952. Neumann and his wife Kitty (1903–1979) had been friends with Thomas and Katia Mann since the 1920s, when they lived in the same neighbourhood as the Manns. In 1933 the Neumanns emigrated first to France and then to Italy, and in 1940 they left for the United States, where they once again ended up living near the Manns. Thomas Mann wrote a memorial address for Neumann which he delivered in Munich on 24 October 1952 (see 'Für Alfred Neumann', in Thomas Mann, *Reden und Aufsätze* II, *GW* X, p. 530f.). The Mann–Neumann correspondence, edited by Peter de Mendelssohn, appeared in Heidelberg in 1977. It seems likely that Adorno had met Alfred Neumann through Thomas Mann in the American years.

3 Max Horkheimer was elected rector of the University of Frankfurt on 20 November 1950 and served until 1953.

4 The talk 'The Artist and Society'. See Letter 32, note 4.

5 Adorno is probably alluding to his study *Zur Metakritik der Erkenntnistheorie: Studien über Husserl und die phänomenologischen Antinomien*, which was published in Stuttgart in 1956. The first, second and fourth chapters were based on the studies of Husserl which Adorno had already written in Oxford between 1934 and 1937. The work has appeared in English with the title *Against Epistemology*, translated by Willis Domingo (Oxford, 1982).

Zurich 30. X. 52

Dear Dr Adorno,

Not knowing your precise address, I have directed these lines via the publisher who sent me a copy of the 'Wagner'. I have been reading it for days with the greatest sense of urgency. It is a tremendous book, fascinating for its perspicacious intimacy with an object which, for all of your *enforced* admiration (unintentionally breaking through now and again), still reveals itself as one of the greatest and spiritually liberating things that has ever presented itself to critical reflection. The most authoritative chapter is surely that on the instrumentation,[1] which is itself so closely connected with 'phantasmagoria', with the 'concealment of the productive process through the appearing product', as the governing principle of Wagnerian form.[2] These pages have clearly shown me the degree to which I am a Wagnerian – and to which I am *not*. I have followed Wagner's example in many respects, I have 'recalled' his works in many ways. But the illusionistic character of a work of art that would present itself as reality is entirely alien to me and has never fired my artistic ambitions. My own relationship to the 'work' itself was always too honestly ironical for that, and I have always taken pleasure in compromising the act of production in some humoristic fashion or other.

But that is all by the by. Your book is *enormously interesting* on every page. I have made innumerable pencil jottings in the text, and some minor queries as well.[3] One of these concerns 'the singing voice is detached from the life of music and its logic: to sing a motif would conflict with the requirement of natural intonation.'[4] This does not seem to be entirely true. Quite a few motifs are sung, the most striking example being the 'Annunciation' addressed to Sieglinde:[5] 'For know one thing, and remember it indeed: the noblest hero of the world you bear, O woman, within your sheltering womb.' Another example would be Alberich's curse upon the gold,[6] which, like Lohengrin's injunction 'Never shalt thou ask', clearly shows how a motif is often sung first, before the orchestra then takes it up again in various reminiscences. In the 'Liebestod' Isolde also sings a good part of the melody[7] (from Act II), although it is true that subsequently the voice merely follows 'the harmonies of the orchestra'. And there are other cases.

Most of all I was impressed by the pages towards the end on Wagner's work as an expression of incipient decay of the bourgeois world. 'There is not a single decadent moment in Wagner's work from which productive insight could not extract the forces of change.'[8] That reveals very great insight, as does the remark about 'the neurotic's ability to contemplate his own decadence and to transcend it'.[9] And likewise the *question*: 'whether Nietzsche's criterion of health[10] is of greater benefit than the critical consciousness that Wagner's grandiose weakness acquires in his commerce with all the unconscious forces responsible for his own decadence ... the bourgeois nihilist sees through the nihilism of the age that will follow his own.' This is superb! And then the remarkably prophetic quotation from 'Religion and Art'.[11]

'However, if a decadent society develops the seeds of the society that will perhaps one day take its place . . .'[12] If there were only a single positive word, my honoured friend, that vouchsafed even the vaguest glimpse of the true society which we are forced to postulate! In this respect, and only this, your own reflections from damaged life[13] say nothing. But what is right here, what would be right here? On one occasion you quote Lukács with approval,[14] and much of what you say suggests a kind of purified communism. But then what is *that*? The Russian despotism is a mistake. But is communism really conceivable without despotism? 'It's not this, and it's not that. But what – what then will it be in the end??', as Michael Kramer says.[15]

The terror of late bourgeois society and that of the 'new' society stand armed to the teeth over against each other and at any moment everything might 'through some incalculable error just go up in smoke'.[16] All that I can see approaching, spreading and irresistibly advancing upon us, is barbarism. Our higher literature strikes me as little but a hasty résumé and *parodic* recapitulation of the western myth before the final onset of the night. How many of us are there now who can still 'recognize' the 'fundamental experiences of the bourgeois era',[17] can still understand the passage where the horn 'catches the echo of the shepherd's melancholy song'? We are fast shrinking in number and already find ourselves surrounded by masses who can no longer 'recognize' anything. May heaven grant us something of that productive energy which can wrest fresh moments of the new from every moment of decay!

Yours,
Thomas Mann

SOURCE: O: MS; Theodor W. Adorno Archive, Frankfurt am Main. Fp: *Briefe III*, p. 274ff.

1 See GS 13, pp. 68–81: chapter 5 on 'Colour'; English translation: *In Search of Wagner* (London, 1981), pp. 71–84.

2 See GS 13, p. 82; *In Search of Wagner*, chapter 6, p. 85.

3 Mann's copy of Adorno's book is preserved in the Thomas Mann Archive.

4 The passage of Adorno's book to which Thomas Mann is critically alluding here runs as follows: 'The very attempt to adapt the arts to each other disrupts the unity of the compositional structure. The *Sprechgesang* was the means devised by Wagner to guarantee such unity. The idea was that a quasi-natural intonation would harmonize music and language without doing violence to either. But this had the effect that the singing voice, the as it were palpable bearer of the musical action, the universal object of attention at the opera, is separated by force from the actual musical content. Apart from the few passages in which the dominance of the musical form can be conceded, the singing voice is detached from the life of music and its logic: to sing a motif would conflict with the requirement of natural intonation and would depart from the normal inflections of speech. In Wagner's music the most vital elements, song and orchestra, necessarily diverge . . . Song, the most immediate of the two, ceases to be involved in the most essential part, the thematic texture, except in the abstract and non-committal sense that the singing voice follows the orchestral harmonies' (*GS* 13, p. 98; *In Search of Wagner*, p. 103).

5 The precise text of the original reads: 'Denn eines wisse / und wahr' es immer: / den hehrsten Helden der Welt / hegst du, o Weib, / im schirmenden Schoos!' (see *Die Walküre*, Act III, scene 1).

6 See *Das Rheingold*, scene 1: 'Das Licht lösch'ich euch aus, / entreisse dem Riff das Gold, / schmiede den rächenden Ring: / denn hör'es die Fluth – / so verfluch' ich die Liebe!' [I shall quench your light, / wrest the gold from the rock, / and forge the avenging ring: / let the waters hear me – for thus do I curse Love!']

7 *Tristan und Isolde*, Act III, scene 3.

8 See *GS* 13, p. 143; *In Search of Wagner*, p. 153.

9 See *GS* 13, p. 144; *In Search of Wagner*, p. 154.

10 See *GS* 13, p. 144; *In Search of Wagner*, p. 153.

11 See *GS* 13, p. 144; *In Search of Wagner*, p. 155. Adorno cites Wagner's late essay 'Religion und Kunst'. See Richard Wagner, *Gesammelte Schriften und Dichtungen* (Leipzig, 1888), vol. 10, p. 252: '. . . the progress of the art of war has turned away from the springs of moral forces and turned towards the cultivation of mechanical ones: here the rawest forces of the lower powers of nature are transformed into an artificial play in which, for all the arithmetic and mathematics involved, the blind will could one day break its leash and reveal itself with elemental force. Already a grim and ghostly spectacle is afforded by the iron-clad Monitors against which the stately sailing ships are helpless: mute and obedient men, who no longer look like men, serve these monsters and will never desert their appalling boiler rooms. But just as in nature everything has its own destructive foe, so art invents torpedoes for the sea and dynamite for everywhere else. It is quite conceivable that everything, together with art and science, honour and valour, life and property, might one day, through some incalculable error, just go up in smoke.'

12 See *GS* 13, p. 143; *In Search of Wagner*, p. 153.

13 Thomas Mann is alluding to the subtitle of Adorno's book of aphorisms *Minima Moralia.*

14 Adorno mentions Lukács in connection with a citation from Wagner's biographer C. P. Glasenapp: 'In the *Ring* the victory of society over the opposition and the recruitment of the latter for bourgeois purposes is idealized into a transcendental fate. Such an idealization alienates the allegory of world history from the actual historical process: "What he had wanted to show was the inevitable decline of the world in its previous historical phase and to contrast this with Siegfried, the fearless, joyful man of the future. But as he came to carry out his plan, and indeed even in its initial conception, he was compelled to recognize that unconsciously he had been pursuing another and much deeper idea. What he had perceived in his poem, and what he has recognized in its essential senselessness, was not just a single phase of world history, but the nature of the world as such in all its conceivable phases." This is a textbook example of what Lukács once described as trivialization through profundity: by levelling down to the plane of the universally human and its "senselessness", the true "essence" of society – its actual historical laws of movement – is overlooked and the tragedy of a specific historical is diluted into a universal historical principle.' See *GS* 13, p. 131; *In Search of Wagner*, pp. 139–40.

15 The precise wording of the lines at the end of Gerhart Hauptmann's drama reads: 'It is not this, and it is not that, but what [. . .] – what will it really be in the end???'

16 See the end of the long quotation from Wagner's essay 'Religion und Kunst', note 11 above.

17 Mann is alluding to the following remarks: 'The passage in Act III of Tristan, where the horn in the orchestra soars above the boundary separating "nothingness" and "something" and catches the echo of the melancholy song as Tristan stirs – that passage will survive as long as the fundamental experiences of the bourgeois era can still be felt by human beings. Together with the other passage, the scene of Brünnhilde's awakening, it is evidence of that glimmering awareness without which the concept of nothingness, or so Wagner's music would have us believe, could never be conceived.' See *GS* 13, p. 141; *In Search of Wagner*, p. 151.

35   THEODOR W. ADORNO TO THOMAS MANN
     SANTA MONICA, 1.12.1952

T. W. Adorno
803 Yale Str.
Santa Monica, Calif.

1 December 1952

My dear and esteemed Dr Mann,
     Your letter proved a greater joy than I can express, not merely as the first and most important response to the book on Wagner, and not

merely for the encouraging confirmation it suggests, but even more because of your own authentic contribution to the question. I do not really know how to thank you, and may perhaps best do so by trying to respond to what you have said.

The line you draw between Wagner and yourself is not a purely individual matter, it seems to me, but a historical-philosophical one. If one may resort to concepts that have been ruined by historians of literature and culture, one would have to say that a certain romantic aestheticism still naively survives in Wagner, as in some ways it does in Baudelaire, an undiminished faith in the work of art as something self-sufficient and meaningfully real. But in them, and similarly also in Gide, this aestheticism comes to self-consciousness and transcends itself from within without the external support of any 'Weltanschauung'. And it is Nietzsche who surely marks this threshold: on the one hand he retained the Wagnerian conception of the work of art throughout his life (recently I came across this formulation in Nietzsche: an anti-metaphysical world-view, yes, but an artistic one),[1] while on the other hand he could also formulate the thought that the work of art should not appear as if it were created at all.[2] The latter formulation can be found in almost exactly the same words in Valéry. And I sometimes suspect that this, admittedly transformed, legacy of aestheticism, as a repudiation of the realm of ends and purposes, is the only effective remedy for the spreading barbarism we see around us; and if the origins of the disaster cannot be sought simply in the developmental tendencies of bourgeois society, but can also be traced to the characteristic outlook of its critics, then we must consider this issue first of all. Perhaps it was the inconspicuous weakness of Marx, though one of the implications of which can hardly be exaggerated, that he did not truly and substantially embody in himself the culture against which he struggled. His language, particularly in the period of his maturity, strongly suggests something of the kind. And when he effectively dissolves the tension between the utopian and positivist elements of his thought in favour of the latter, thus anticipating the way in which socialism itself would eventually become another part of the machinery of production, this is surely connected with a curious blindness to the moment of semblance without which there can be no truth. I fear that this is where the Church Fathers of dialectical materialism proved to be all too bourgeois themselves, and if you spoke once of an ideal socialist who would understand something of Hölderlin,[3] you must surely have had something similar in mind. But one can hardly say this sort of thing today without inviting misunderstanding, and if one does say it, one is immediately likely to be misused by those who simply claim to defend culture against materialism.

May I respond, at the risk of pedantry, to one of your objections? It concerns my theory that the *leading* voice, and that is to say, the singing voice, is excluded from the motivic life of the work and thus from the principal matter of musical interest. Of course, you are quite right, there appears to be no lack of examples to the contrary, and if I remember correctly I was not attempting to mount a universal and exclusive claim here (I do not have a copy of the text to hand). But these passages have a particular and exceptional character of their own, as do the properly polyphonic passages which I discussed. When the singing voice does present specific motifs, they always have a certain extra-territoriality about them, as in cases of express citation or magical invocation. In addition to the ones you mention, one can find other examples, such as the line 'Durch Mitleid wissend, der reine Tor' [Made wise through pity, the pure fool].[4] The singing voice presents the motifs when the subject itself does not speak, but rather when some oracle, command or prophecy speaks through the subject; and it is precisely in this sense that the measures proclaiming 'the noblest hero of the world' are to be understood. And if I am not mistaken, this is the only occasion in which the Siegfried motif itself is anticipated in the 'Walküre'. Of course, the situation is rather different with the equally motivic melody that is sung in the 'Liebestod', but this is one of those releasing and redeeming 'pieces' which the later Wagner wisely and repeatedly inserted into the music dramas as a kind of antithesis which functions precisely to suspend the overall stylistic principle. But all this represents an element of opposition and only acquires significance in relation to the prevailing and effectively constitutive musical procedure upon which I concentrated my analysis. I have no doubt that you will actually agree with me in this respect.

Yet I am rather less able to answer your other fundamental objection, the question concerning the positive, for here all I can say is that only a rogue gives more than he has. If anything in Hegel, and in those who turned him right way up,[5] has become part of my very flesh and blood, it is an asceticism with regard to any unmediated expression of the positive. This truly is a case of asceticism, believe me, since the opposite impulse, a tendency to the unfettered expression of hope, really lies much closer to my own nature. But I have the constant feeling that we are merely encouraging the cause of untruth if we turn prematurely to the positive and fail to persevere in the negative. And this has powerfully impressed itself upon me once again over the last few days when I stumbled upon George's 'Seventh Ring'[6] as I was unpacking a quantity of books here. Like Nietzsche, he was incapable of persevering in the negative and was driven to create a god for himself which was simply an idol. The result was not merely the comic spectacle of solemn cultic masquerade, but, rather more importantly, the fact that George, at least after 'The Carpet', effectively destroyed himself as an artist – he simply attempted, out of his own resources, to fashion forms of aesthetic validity which, being objectively invalid, inevitably disintegrated in his hands. And this eventually gave rise to the wretched spoken choruses in 'The Star'[7] and a cult of 'leadership' which was not really as remote from the fascistic version of the idea as the high-minded George himself liked to believe. Now I have no wish to encourage the twilight of the idols to the point of fetishizing determinate negation itself, and if it is true that the power of the positive has now passed over to the negative, it is no less true that negation draws its rights solely from the power of the positive. Whether it is possible to express this directly in our own time, as we should ultimately have to do, or whether ascesis will have to have the final word, I cannot tell – for all that I have been accustomed throughout my life to stare into the dark. In a corner of my heart I do still believe this will one day be possible. But I would also ask, *en attendant*, whether in the end this whole question concerning the positive and the negative does not harbour a false, and massively inflated, problem which, through its very abstractness, merely encourages us to lose sight of what is essential here. For utopia is the concrete, and not itself some universal theory or finished recommendation for praxis. And every really fulfilled intuition, which also indeed involves the conceptual dimension, is an earnest of precisely what would otherwise fall helpless victim to the grinding of principles. But then saying this to you, as an artist, is like bearing owls, that take their flight only with the falling of the dusk,[8] to Athens.

But a consoling reflection for now. This feeling of 'we are the last', to which your letter gave such painful and emphatic expression, already has a long history of its own. You are even more familiar than I with similar utterances in the later Goethe, in Baudelaire, in Nietzsche, in Karl Kraus, and the thread is still not entirely broken in spite of everything. And can it ever break while humanity not merely rages against itself, but also continues to reproduce its own existence? If I have kept anything heartening from my years in Germany it is the confirmation of this very thought, the experience that the regression to barbarism is not entirely what we are often enough tempted to believe. Even the thesis of the demise of culture has weakened its hold for me through contact with the younger people with whom we are now able to work. From the depths of my heart I hope that your return to Europe will also vouchsafe you something of the consolation which now sustains me. Permit me to add, a few weeks after my return here, that only now do I fully understand your own decision in this matter and am rather ashamed that I ever counselled you otherwise.

To indicate something of the lie of the land, I also enclose the critical review by Herr Stuckenschmidt[9] which also subtly tries to play you off against me. Since every feature of my book, which may certainly have its defects, is closely developed from a central perspective, the last thing I had expected was to stand accused of a merely 'associative' approach to the subject. But then the alliance of slyness and cunning can accomplish much, and his criticism appeals so obviously to the prevailing spirit of the time that it may well create a lot of trouble.

With the most grateful respect,

Your faithful,

Teddie Adorno

SOURCE: O: TS with handwritten corrections; Thomas Mann Archive, Zurich.

1 The precise wording of the original is: 'An anti-metaphysical conception of the world – yes, but an artistic one' (see Friedrich Nietzsche, *Werke in drei Bänden*, ed. Karl Schlechta, vol. 3, Darmstadt, 1982, p. 481 [from the *Nachlass* of the 1880s]).

2 Adorno is probably alluding to *Human, All Too Human*, Part 4: 'From the Soul of Artists and Writers', Aphorism 145: '*Perfection said not to have evolved*. . . . The artist knows that his work has its full effect only when it arouses belief in an improvisation, in a wondrous instantaneousness of origin; and so he encourages this illusion and introduces into art elements of inspired unrest, of blindly groping disorder, of expectantly attentive dreaming when creation begins, as deceptions that dispose the soul of the viewer or listener to believe in the sudden emergence of perfection.' Paul Valéry (1871–1945) had written in the foreword to the catalogue of an exhibition of works by the impressionist painter Berthe Morisot (1841–1895): 'she ceaselessly pursued the noble tasks of the proudest and most elect art, that art which is fulfilled entirely in the zeal to achieve, through countless efforts which we produce and destroy without pity, the impression that the miracle of this creation has sprung from nothing, fully accomplished at a single stroke' (Paul Valéry, 'Tante Berthe', in *Werke*, Vol. 6: *Zur Ästhetik und Philosophie der Künste*, ed. Jürgen Schmidt-Radefeldt, Frankfurt am Main and Leipzig, 1995, pp. 394–9, the passage in question, p. 394). Adorno interpreted this aphorism of Nietzsche in an aphorism of his own in *Minima Moralia* (number 145).

3 In his essay 'Goethe and Tolstoy' of 1921 Thomas Mann had claimed: '[Socialism] is today, from a political perspective, our real national party; but it will not truly be capable of accomplishing its national task until, to put it very pointedly, Karl Marx has come to read Hölderlin, an encounter which already seems as if it is about to transpire' (*Reden und Aufsätze* I, GW IX, p. 170). In 1927 Mann returned to this idea in his essay 'Culture and Socialism': 'What is urgently needed, what could definitively be called German, would be a pact and alliance between the conservative idea of culture and the

revolutionary concept of society, between Greece and Moscow, to put it force-fully – I have already attempted to formulate this incisively before. I said that things would only go well with Germany, that the country would only truly find itself, if Karl Marx were able to read Friedrich Hölderlin – an encounter which is already about to transpire. I forgot to add that an appropriation from one side alone would merely prove fruitless' (Thomas Mann, *Essays*, ed. Hermann Kurzke and Stephan Stachorski, Vol. 3: *Ein Appell an die Vernunft, 1926–1933*, Frankfurt am Main, 1994, p. 63).

4 In Act I of Wagner's *Parsifal* the figure of Amfortas prophesies the coming of Parsifal as a 'pure fool' who is 'made wise through pity'.

5 Adorno is alluding to the critique of Hegelian idealism in Karl Marx and Friedrich Engels: 'We interpreted the concepts in our heads materialistically in turn as the reflections of real things, instead of interpreting the real things as reflections of this or that level of the absolute concept [. . .] The dialectic of concepts itself thereby became simply the conscious reflection of the dialec-tical movement of the real world, and the Hegelian dialectic was thereby turned on its head or, rather, was turned from the head where it stood back on its feet once again.' (See Friedrich Engels, *Ludwig Feuerbach und der Ausgang des klassischen deutschen Philosophie*, in Karl Marx and Friedrich Engels, *Werke*, vol. 21, Berlin, 1962, p. 293.)

6 The poetic cycles *Der siebente Ring* (1907–9) and *Der Teppich des Lebens* (1899–1901) by Stefan George (1868–1933).

7 Adorno is referring to Stefan George's collection *Der Stern des Bundes* of 1913–14. Envisaged by George as a kind of 'esoteric book', it nonetheless became a favourite work with young soldiers at the front in the First World War.

8 Adorno is alluding to the preface of the *Philosophy of Right*, where Hegel says: 'One word more about giving instruction as to what the world ought to be. Philosophy in any case always comes on the scene too late to give it. As the thought of the world, it appears only when actuality is already there cut and dried after its process of formation has been completed. The teaching of the concept, which is also history's inescapable lesson, is that it is only when actuality is mature that the ideal first appears over against the real and that the ideal apprehends this same real world in its substance and builds it up for itself into the shape of an intellectual realm. When philosophy paints its grey in grey, then has a shape of life grown old. By philosophy's grey in grey it cannot be rejuvenated, but only understood. The owl of Minerva spreads its wings only with the falling of the dusk' (*Hegel's Philosophy of Right*, trans. T. M. Knox, Oxford, 1967, pp. 12–13).

9 In his review of Adorno's book on Wagner (in the *Neue Zeitung* of 8–9 November 1952) Hans Heinz Stuckenschmidt had also alluded to Thomas Mann's famous speech *The Sufferings and Greatness of Richard Wagner*: 'Criticism of Wagner has once again, and especially today, become a matter of some importance, and one may be grateful to Adorno that he has provided such an unsparing example. The general intellectual ambience of his critique

often resembles that of Thomas Mann's fine speech on Wagner from 1933, as when he points out the affinity between Wagner's sensuous orchestral colour and the "Letters to a Seamstress". But he goes further than Mann in revealing Wagner's bizarre relationship to the sexual dimension of experience. Whether it was right and perceptive of the author to evaluate this empirically correct information by reference to the concept of "syphiliphobia" on the other hand is perhaps something which the real Wagnerians alone can decide.'

36 THEODOR W. ADORNO TO THOMAS MANN
   FRANKFURT AM MAIN, 18.1.1954

T. W. Adorno   Frankfurt a. M., 18 January 1954
                                Kettenhofweg 123

My dear and esteemed Dr Mann,

My unduly extended delay in responding to 'The Betrayed One' is owing entirely to the fact that I wished to read it with that unhurried leisure which it would seem almost blasphemous to deny the work – and to become acquainted with your text as the instalments gradually appeared in 'Merkur'.[1] But in the event this proved impossible. I have at last found the required peace and quiet during the winter vacation, and would now like to express my gratitude and admiration for your scandalous parable. You have drawn forth such an abundance of things from the theme of the entwinement of eros and death, and you have done it so concretely and with such a wealth of images. You have permitted the metaphorical character of the whole to illuminate the work throughout in a truly masterly fashion, without striving to produce what the German aestheticians call 'the symbolic', which is to say, without attempting to conceal the parable-like character, the surplus of thought over the material, which is properly demanded today. There can be no end of praise for the subtleties and concentrated experiences that have found their way into the work, such as the broken manner in which alone we can now experience nature ('when the avenues become poetical').[2] Or the careful manner in which you have introduced a smaller allegory within the context of a greater, like the little second hand within the clock face, that of the musky odour of the heap of excrement.[3] You have surely never succeeded better in bringing the scandalous power of the forbidden into such close connection with the central theme itself through the coquettish shamelessness with which you treat the facts of life[4] that effectively constitute the parable – an intention that delicately pervades the whole, the stamping club foot and the painful pardon included. As I read the text

I was powerfully reminded of the musical technique of variation, and I flatter myself that such a thought was not so far from your own mind either, that you have offered us a variation of your fundamental theme in which light and dark, forte and piano, and any other oppositions we might imagine, had precisely changed places with one another: what finds expression here is not the life which yearns for death, but rather the death which yearns for life, and this latter also precisely represents the uncomprehended and the impermissible which shatters the sphere of social immanence – so much so that the majority of your readers, confronted with this late work, like the wand of some scurrilous Circe, will seem transformed into maiden aunts wielding aloft the gladius dei.[5]

Bourgeois civilization has repressed all that is 'horrific' in death, trying either to ennoble it or to corral it with hygiene. The futility of false life must not be allowed to enter consciousness through the ghastliness that death reveals – nor the fact that death is an offence to human beings, one that should be abolished rather than celebrated in the name of tragedy. The shock your story provokes infringes all the accepted rules of play. And in this alone there is something infinitely liberating. One can truly say that with this story you have finally taken the old Schopenhauerian theme of delusion, of the experienced deceptiveness and futility of life, to a rigorously materialist conclusion that spells an end to ideological fantasy. And the contrast between this intention and the boldly artificial means that you have adopted to pursue it only serves to reinforce this effect. You drive the tension between culture and what culture itself conceals to a breaking point, to a point of dialectical reversal. The sovereign freedom with which you treat the entire humanistic tradition, that as its authentic bearer you nonetheless sustain, is quite magnificent. I believe that the wealth that is harboured within this truly incommensurable work will only gradually reveal itself over time.

I cannot resist sharing a little detail with which you may be unfamiliar. If Rosalie encouraged her daughter to pursue abstraction by trying to paint atmosphere itself,[6] I have to say this has been done even before you suggested it. For it seems to my eye, which lacks expertise for the technical aspects of painting, as if the recent works of the surrealist Masson,[7] whom I met in Paris about a year ago, possess the very atmosphere of Renoir's art, although all reference to particular objects has vanished. And over there they do make a direct connection between the most radical forms of painting and the earlier impressionistic tendencies. And if I am not mistaken, it seems that Monet ultimately displays a similar tendency to dissolve all representational elements, not to mention certain musical parallels such as Debussy's 'Jeux' for example.[8] If you do make it to Paris – and I can hardly

102

imagine that your labours on 'Krull' can tolerate too protracted an absence from this his chosen homeland – you must not fail to pay a visit to the Leiris Gallery,[9] and allow my really charming friend Kahnweiler to show you these paintings by Masson. This will at least justify Rosalie in regarding herself in your eyes as more advanced than the rather strict Anna.

If I have any criticism to make, it certainly does not spring from any reservations whatsoever about the work as such, but is prompted by a critical concept which has already occupied me for many years and which you may also be interested to consider. Unless I am mistaken, the figure of Ken displays all the characteristics of an American of the late forties or fifties, rather than the twenties. You will naturally be able to judge this much more precisely than I can. Now of course one could always argue that this reflects the artist's legitimate freedom to shape his own material, and that strictly chronological fidelity is an extremely subordinate consideration here, even where the fine detail of accurate human depiction is concerned. But I merely wonder whether this seemingly self-evident argument is as strong as it appears. If you set a work in the twenties, if you allow the story to unfold after the first war rather than after the second, then you will have your own good reasons for this – most obviously the fact that it is impossible to imagine an existence like that of Frau von Tümmler in the context of today. But then one thereby contracts a kind of artistic obligation, rather as one does with the very first bar of a piece of music. Not indeed an obligation to external fidelity in matters of 'historical colour', but one which does ensure that the images evoked in the work of art are also, at the same time, historical. And here, unless I am much mistaken, we stumble upon the paradoxical circumstance that the evocation of such artistic images – the genuinely aesthetic desideratum – is all the more perfectly realized the more authentic these realistic elements are. One might almost claim that one's own subjective investment in the material does not stand, as our culture and history tend to suggest, in any simple opposition to the demand for realism which indeed, in a certain sense, resounds throughout your work. The more precisely one keeps to the historical details of specific types of human individuals, the more one may realize the spiritual character of the material and establish the power of the imago. It was the reading of Proust that first prompted these errant reflections, and they have only been strongly reinforced once again by perusal of 'The Betrayed One'. It seems to me at present as if such precision might do something to atone for the sin that is a moment of all artistic fiction, as if this sin might itself be cured by means of the most exact imagination. But I am hardly sure whether these stammering words have remotely managed to communicate what hovers before my mind's eye, and not rather provoked the suspicion that I have fallen helpless victim to the professorial mentality and stand myself in need of cure.

'The Chosen One' and 'The Betrayed One', it seems to me, appear almost by their very titles to suggest a certain cyclical relationship. May we perhaps hope for a third story of this kind, just as Plato, if he and Wilamowitz[10] have not deceived us, originally intended to supplement 'The Sophist' and 'The Statesman' with 'The Philosopher'? Or are you now once again entirely absorbed in 'Krull'? I have heard all kinds of welcome and encouraging things about your progress in this respect from our dear friend Hirsch.[11] But I should be profoundly grateful if you could possibly drop me a line about this yourself. Perhaps you have found time to glance at my essay on Kafka,[12] with the proofs of which I burdened you a couple of months ago and which should at least absolve me from the suspicion of being all too professorial.

I do now hope that we shall be able to meet very soon. I don't know what your current plans are, but we are certainly intending to spend August in the Engadine. I am already taking steps to avoid all the work sessions, vacation courses and similar nuisances that otherwise threaten to frustrate our plans. But Graubünden is very close to Zurich and, if this is convenient for you and will not keep you from anything more important, there should be nothing to prevent us meeting then.

With heartfelt admiration,

Your faithful,

Teddie Adorno

SOURCE: O: TS with handwritten corrections; Thomas Mann Archive, Zurich. Pp: Theodor W. Adorno, 'Aus einem Brief über die "Betrogene"', *Akzente* 2 (1955), pp. 284–7.

1 See Thomas Mann, *Die Betrogene* [The Betrayed One], *Merkur* 7 (1953), pp. 401–17, 549–73, 657–72. The novel was published in book form in Frankfurt am Main in the same year. See *GW* VIII, pp. 877–950. It was translated into English under the title *The Black Swan*, trans. W. R. Trask (London, 1954).

2 The passage Adorno is referring to reads as follows: 'The season of flowering trees, when the roads became poetic, when the dear familiar landscape of their walks clothed itself in charming, white and rosy promise of fruit – what a bewitching time!' (*Die Betrogene*, *GW* VIII, p. 884; English translation: *The Black Swan*, p. 17).

3 In the story Rosalie and her daughter Anna, who was afflicted at birth with a club foot, are out walking together when they become aware of the odour: 'Strolling along between fields and the edge of a wood, they suddenly noticed an odour of musk, at first almost imperceptibly faint, then stronger. It was Rosalie who first sniffed it and expressed her awareness by an "Oh! Where

does that come from?" but her daughter soon had to concur: Yes, there was some sort of odour, and, yes, it did seem to be definable as musky – there was no doubt about it. Two steps sufficed to bring them within sight of its source, which was repellent. It was there by the roadside, seething in the sun, with blowflies covering it and flying all around it – a little mound of excrement, which they preferred not to investigate more closely. The small area represented a meeting-ground of animal, or perhaps human faeces, with some sort of putrid vegetation, and the greatly decomposed body of some small woodland creature seemed to be present too. In short, nothing could be nastier than the teeming little mound; but its evil effluvium, which drew the blowflies by hundreds, was, in its ambivalence, no longer to be called a stench but must undoubtedly be pronounced the odour of musk.' (GW VIII, p. 887; *The Black Swan*, pp. 22–3.)

4 The words 'facts of life' are in English in the original.

5 Adorno is alluding to Thomas Mann's early story *Gladius Dei* of 1902.

6 Adorno is referring to the following passage from the novel: 'And she seriously proposed to her that if she was set upon transposition and absolutely must be abstract, she should try, at least once, to express odours in colour.

This idea came to her late in June, when the lindens were in flower – again for her the one lovely time of the year, when for a week or two the avenues of trees outside filled the whole house, through the open windows, with the indescribably pure and mild, enchanting odour of their late bloom, and the smile of rapture never faded from Rosalie's lips. It was then that she said: "That is what you painters should paint, try your artistry on that! You don't want to banish Nature from art entirely; actually you always start from her in your abstractions, and you need something sensory in order to intellectualize it. Now odour, if I may say so, is sensory and abstract at the same time, we don't see it, it speaks to us ethereally. And it ought to fascinate you to convey an invisible felicity to the sense of sight, on which after all, the art of painting rests.' (GW VIII, p. 886; *The Black Swan*, p. 21.)

7 The French painter André Masson (1896–1987) was associated with the surrealist movement between 1924 and 1928.

8 Adorno is referring to the ballet score by Claude Debussy (1862–1918). The music was composed in 1912 and the ballet was performed in 1913.

9 Daniel-Henry Kahnweiler (1884–1979) organized the first special exhibition of Masson's works in 1923 in his gallery, the Galerie Simon, in Paris. During the German occupation of France, when Kahnweiler was forced to remain in hiding, the gallery was run by Louise Leiris (1902–1988), the illegitimate daughter of his wife, Lucie Godon (1882–1945). After the war the gallery was renamed after Louise Leiris.

10 The classical scholar Ulrich von Wilamowitz-Moellendorff (1848–1931) had argued that Plato had originally planned a tetralogy of dialogues, with the *Theaetetus* conceived as the introductory exposition of the argument. Wilamowitz claimed therefore that what we actually possess is effectively 'the

torso of a new masterwork': 'He only managed to finish the twinned dialogues of *The Sophist* and *The Statesman*, which were certainly brought out together. For the latter text explicitly alludes to *The Sophist* at 284b. But both of them were written on the assumption that the final dialogue of the group, *The Philosopher*, was about to appear, since they refer to this as well (*The Sophist* 253e and *The Statesman* 257a).' (See Ulrich von Wilamowitz-Moellendorff, *Platon: Sein Leben und Werke*, based on the author's third edition, ed. Bruno Snell, Berlin and Frankfurt am Main, 1948, p. 439.)

11 The art historian Rudolf Hirsch (1905–1996), who had emigrated to Holland in 1933, was employed in the editorial office of the Bermann-Fischer-Querido Verlag in Amsterdam in 1948. At Gottfried Bermann Fischer's request Hirsch took over as literary editor of Fischer Verlag in 1950 and also became principal editor of *Die Neue Rundschau* in Frankfurt am Main. From 1954 until 1962 Hirsch was the director of Fischer Verlag.

12 See Adorno, 'Aufzeichnungen zu Kafka', *Die Neue Rundschau*, 64 (1953), pp. 325–53; *GS* 10.1, pp. 254–87; English translation: 'Notes on Kafka', *Prisms*, trans. Samuel Weber and Shierry Weber (London, 1967), pp. 243–71.

37 THOMAS MANN TO THEODOR W. ADORNO
    ERLENBACH, 8.3.1954

THOMAS MANN   Erlenbach-Zürich

                                                              8.III.54

Dear Dr Adorno,

I still owe you a proper reply for the fine and significant letter with which you surprised me on the subject of 'The Betrayed One'. The letter actually accompanied me to Italy,[1] where we have spent four weeks in refuge from the murderous cold over here. But while we were there, in Sicily, Rome, Florence and Milan, I found time only to read it over and over again, rather than to express my gratitude for your intellectual sympathy with an idiotically 'controversial' work whose failure can only lie in its very existence. For if it is really there, it cannot be any different from what it is. The stylization of the work has provoked more offence, it seems to me, than the 'delicate' subject matter itself. But it was always part of the original conception that this crass case of nature-demonism (an anecdote from the domain of reality) would have to be treated in a pre-realist manner rather in the style of a classical novella. The language of the theatre should surely reflect now the way in which Rosalie (an intentionally comic name; the figure is actually half-comically conceived) and Anna talk to one another!

Then people would certainly listen. Realism is no longer capable of yielding any enjoyment.

It was quite remarkable to behold how your own incredibly developed critical style, a dagger that goes straight to the heart of things, can be so powerfully applied even in the private context of a letter to matters of such concern to me. The style fascinates me wherever I encounter it. I have read not merely your imaginative reflections on Kafka, but, as I believe, everything else of yours which has recently appeared in journals in one place or another,[2] and that is quite a lot. Only now is it becoming clear that you were really half-silent during the years in America, and that Europe has enormously encouraged your own productive work by providing you with so many fresh and different possibilities. And this now really resembles a kind of 'motus animi continuus'[3] which has impressed me again and again in my own state of weariness (for I am indeed very weary).

For the rest journals are terrible things – confusing, time-wasting, disheartening. The 'literary world' as such is dreadful and destructive, one should simply ignore it and preserve one's privacy before the market-clamour of clever gossip. The discovery of good particular books is another matter of course. Thus I have derived great enjoyment from the already justly celebrated 'Memoirs of Hadrian' by Yourcenar,[4] a masterpiece of eruditely researched fiction, as beautiful as it is convincing. And I have now started reading the biography of Nietzsche by R. Blunck,[5] and the first volume (there will be three) appears to promise an accurate and devotedly true account. For the rest, exposure to the most recent and remarkable products of the Joycean, and post-Joycean, world,[6] such as 'En attendant Godot', can only divert me at best – and I cannot help feeling some anxiety for the society that finds acclaimed expression in such a work. It has received countless performances in Paris, and to great applause when a figure on stage cries out to the public: 'what a swamp!' The 'opposition' is surely right to speak of 'end-works' in this connection – if only its own products were not so hopelessly unengaging and devoid of comedy. But Jacobin virtue cannot produce intrinsically interesting work, and if it is sinful to be interesting, then I am all for sin. And over there, out of pure gratitude, they do not want me to speak out against them, or to speak up for an already fascistic America – in the obscure feeling that whatever future there may be for 'virtue' over there, 'we' at least are doomed.[7]

Germany should certainly be excepted in this regard and where the joy in life that has returned with such incredible vengeance frequently makes me laugh. An amazing people – which for all its efficiency[8] constantly ends up in unhappiness. Once again I feel I can see all this coming. But how obsolete, how overtaken, how refuted my 'Faustus' already looks today if one simply treats it as an allegory of 'Germany'.

We have just this moment returned from Italy, where we experienced a full four weeks of rain. In Taormina I contracted a feverish bronchitis, caused by a cold night in an unheated sleeping-car, which effectively ruined our fortnight there. But a second visit to Rome, a few days in Florence, and a performance of 'Otello' at La Scala have helped to make up for this. As has the remarkable, and almost devoted, understanding that I have encountered in intellectual circles in Italy. This is gratifying, even if one sometimes thinks: children, you are surely mistaken.

We have now bought ourselves a property here, in *Kilchberg*. It is a nice, very suitable house, with a good study for me, lots of room for the library, and convenient connections with the town. We are intending to move in on 1 April. *Alte Landstrasse 39*. This will be my final address, as I hope. There has been so much change and travel during these last few years of my life.

With my best wishes,

Yours,

Thomas Mann

SOURCE: O: MS with printed letterhead; Theodor W. Adorno Archive, Frankfurt am Main. Pp: *Tagebücher 1953–1955*, p. 577.

1 The Manns were in Italy from 4 February until 4 March. They started in Rome and travelled on to Taormina in Sicily. They returned to Rome and went on to visit Thomas Mann's youngest daughter, Elisabeth Mann-Borgese, who was then living in Fiesole, near Florence.

2 Apart from a reference to Adorno's 'Notes on Kafka', Thomas Mann's diary entries for 1953 indicate only that he had read Adorno's essay 'Arnold Schönberg 1874–1951', which was first published in *Die Neue Rundschau* (*GS* 101, pp. 152–80; English translation: *Prisms*, London, 1969, pp. 147–72). Other important essays by Adorno that had recently appeared include 'Das Bewusstsein der Wissenssoziologie' (*GS* 10.2, pp. 31–46), 'Veblens Angriff auf die Kultur' (*GS* 10.2, pp. 72–96), 'Zeitlose Mode: Zum Jazz' (*GS* 10.2, pp. 123–37), 'Valéry Proust Museum' (*GS* 10.2, pp. 181–94), 'Der Artist als Statthalter' (*GS* 11, pp. 114–26) and 'Die gegängelte Musik' (*GS* 14, pp. 51–66).

3 Thomas Mann had already appealed to this expression of Cicero's at the beginning of his novella *Death in Venice* in order to describe the artistic productivity of Gustav Aschenbach: 'He was overwrought by a morning of hard, nerve-taxing work, work which never ceased to exact his uttermost in the way of sustained concentration, conscientiousness, and tact; and after the noon meal found himself powerless to check the onward sweep of the productive mechanism within him, that *motus animi continuus* in which, according to

108

Cicero, eloquence resides' (see *Der Tod in Venedig, GW* VIII, p. 444; English translation: *Death in Venice*, trans. H. T. Lowe-Porter, London, 1955, p. 7). In Mann's 'Notebook Number 9', which also contains some preliminary sketches and materials for *Doctor Faustus*, there is an early reference to Cicero's expression, which Mann had first encountered on reading Flaubert's correspondence (the letter to Madame X of 1853). See Thomas Mann, *Notizbücher 7–17*, ed. Hans Wysling and Yvonne Schmidlin, Frankfurt am Main, 1992, p. 151f. And in the later 'Essay on Schiller' Mann writes: 'But what a life this had been! Spent in never-desisting effort, always pushing forward, upward, in a state of motus animi continuus' (see 'Versuch über Schiller', in *Reden und Aufsätze* I, *GW* IX, p. 927; English translation: 'On Schiller', in *Last Essays*, trans. Richard Winston and Clara Winston, London, 1959, p. 68).

4 See Marguerite Yourcenar, *Ich zähmte die Wölfin: Die Errinerungen des Kaisers Hadrian*, trans. Fritz Jaffe (Stuttgart, 1953).

5 See Richard Blunk, *Friedrich Nietzsche: Kindheit und Jugend* (Munich and Basel, 1953). No further volumes actually appeared.

6 See Samuel Beckett, *En attendant Godot* (Paris, 1952). The play was performed for the first time in Paris on 5 January 1953, and the first German performance took place in Berlin on 8 September 1953. Thomas Mann had never seen the play performed but records reading the piece in his diaries (see *Tagebücher 1953–1955*, p. 177f.). Samuel Beckett (1906–1989) had belonged to the circle of James Joyce (1882–1941) in Paris since 1928. Beckett published his essay 'Dante . . . Bruno. Vico . . . Joyce' in Paris in 1929.

7 The word 'doomed' is in English in the original.

8 The word 'efficiency' is in English in the original.

38   THEODOR W. ADORNO TO THOMAS MANN
     FRANKFURT AM MAIN, 8.3.1955

8 March 1955

My dear and esteemed Dr Mann,

It was a great pleasure when Michael[1] called in on us a few days ago – though most distressing to learn that you had not been well for some time,[2] and all the greater our relief on hearing that everything is fine again now. In the meantime I too have suffered from a very bad viral infection with an uncommonly high fever. I still feel extremely weak and am only just beginning to creep about again. And this condition is forcing me, at present, to maintain my intellectual life at a kind of minimum level. I must limit myself here, therefore, to an enquiry which is narrowly and shamefully matter-of-fact, for which you will perhaps forgive me.

A short while back I showed Dr Höllerer,[3] whom you also know, my letter of 18 January last year, in which I attempted to scribble down a few arabesques on the subject of 'The Betrayed One'. Höllerer would like to publish the letter in the issue which 'Akzente' is dedicating to your work. Naturally this can only transpire with your permission, and I would therefore like to ask whether you have any objection – although I should certainly understand if you advised against it through a desire to respect the absolute distinction between general publication and private correspondence. But if you were quite happy for me to publish this material, I should naturally revise the letter to the degree that I could stand by it in literary terms. Would you please be so kind, therefore, as to let me know your own opinion on the matter one way or the other.

I am sure that we shall be able to see each other this year,[4] whether it be in Germany or Switzerland, if you are agreeable, for I cannot adequately express just how much I should look forward to this,

With devoted respect,

And faithfully yours
[Teddie Adorno]

SOURCE: O: TS (carbon copy); Theodor W. Adorno Archive, Frankfurt am Main.

1 The violinist and violist Michael Mann (1919–1977), Thomas Mann's youngest son, and his wife Gret (b. 1916), who were living in Fiesole at the time, were planning to return to Germany and settle in Frankfurt. Michael Mann had sought Adorno's advice about teaching prospects in the field of chamber music and viola-playing at the College of Music in Frankfurt. On 17 February 1955 he was performing in Stuttgart in connection with a radio broadcast, and it was probably shortly afterwards that he visited Adorno in Frankfurt. He was later forced to abandon his musical career for health reasons. He had also studied German language and literature and later taught in the literature department at the University of California between 1962 and 1977.

2 Thomas Mann had travelled to Arosa on 18 January and was staying at the Hotel Excelsior when he contracted a viral infection on 23 January. He was transferred to the hospital in Chur, where he stayed between 31 January and 5 February, and he returned to Kilchberg on 6 February 1955.

3 The writer, essayist and linguist Walter Höllerer (b. 1922) was a member of 'Group 47' and co-editor of Akzente: Zeitschrift für Dichtung between 1954 and 1967. The June issue of 1955 was specifically dedicated to discussions of Thomas Mann's work.

4 In fact Adorno and Mann never met again.

THOMAS MANN   KILCHBERG AM ZÜRICHSEE
                                        ALTE LANDSTRASSE 39

                                          12 March 1955

Dear Dr Adorno,
   It was a pleasure to hear from you, and a pleasure also that
'Akzente' wishes to publish your letter on 'The Betrayed One'.[1] This
is a very good idea to which I have no objection whatsoever, and I can
hardly desire you to revise in detail the fresh and spontaneous character of your letter for the purpose of publication, except insofar as
you would perhaps wish to bring out one or other formulation with
greater literary force. Many foolish things have been said about this
story, and it would be a pity if a private communication of such
significance were to remain hidden from general view.
   So we have been companions in viral illness! What you say about
your own afflictions corresponds precisely with my own experience.
It was a strange vacation I had. I had really put in some work on my
piece on Schiller,[2] and was rather hoping to feel refreshed in Arosa.
And then this happened a few days later. It did not really help to
restore my health up there, so they brought me back down to the cantonal hospital in Chur. And within a week my condition improved so
much that I could recuperate from the recuperation at home. But one
continues to feel these little visitations in one's limbs long after the
event, as you know yourself.
   I am delighted to hear that you are quite sure a reunion will be
possible this year, here or in Germany. I look forward to it as much as
you do,
                            Cordially yours,
                            Thomas Mann

SOURCE: O: TS with handwritten corrections; Theodor W. Adorno Archive,
Frankfurt am Main. Pp: *DüD*, pp. 529 and 554.

1 See Adorno, 'Aus einem Brief über die "Betrogene" an Thomas Mann', in
Akzente 2 (1955), pp. 284–7; *GS* 11, pp. 676–9.

2 See Thomas Mann, *Versuch über Schiller: Zum 150 Todestag des Dichters –
seinem Andenken in Liebe gewidmet.* The essay was written between
13 September 1954 and 10 January 1955 and was published in 1955. See *GW*
IX, pp. 870–951; English translation: 'On Schiller', in *Last Essays*, trans.
Richard Winston and Clara Winston (London, 1959).

May all happiness of spirit be with you in every moment of your life, and our sole thanks for everything you have given us be the wish *ad multos annos*. In everlasting fidelity and heartfelt devotion,

Teddie and Gretel Adorno

SOURCE: Telegram for Thomas Mann's eightieth birthday. Handwritten copy in the Theodor W. Adorno Archive, Frankfurt am Main.

41   THEODOR W. ADORNO TO THOMAS MANN
     FRANKFURT AM MAIN, 28.7.1955

28 July 1955

My dear and esteemed Dr Mann,

I was very disturbed to read in the paper that you were forced to cut short your holiday[1] and return to Switzerland, but I was soon relieved to learn that it was nothing very serious after all. And given my own Satanic inclinations, you will hardly be surprised if a certain element of egoism also played a part in my concern. For there is now even greater hope that I shall get to see you again at last, unless royal hospitality[2] still keeps you in the realm of Peeperkorn.[3] For we are coming to Switzerland on 2 August, and will be at the Waldhaus in Sils Maria on the 3rd, where we plan to spend the rest of the month. And certain rumours have reached me that you too are expected in the Waldhaus. Since you had to break your holiday prematurely, perhaps there is a chance, as soon as you are feeling fully recovered, that you might actually decide to pay a visit up there, even if the said rumours turn out to be false.

So I am writing now in the hope that you may let me know whether there is a chance of meeting in this way. If that should prove impossible, and it were no burden to you, we could seek you out on our way back, as long, of course, as considerations of health do not demand that such intruders be kept at bay.

I still have to thank you very much for the 'Essay on Schiller', which I devoured at night like some detective story, although I was quite unable to find a trace of simple-hearted naivety in it.[4] On the contrary, even you can rarely have written anything so tongue-in-cheek as this. I know no better way of expressing the deep impression the piece has made on me than to single out the passage where you question the concept of the unity of the arts.[5] About a year ago I proposed that one of my students, Joachim Kaiser,[6] some of whose pieces you may have

112

seen, should write a doctoral thesis on this very subject, although nothing has come of it as yet. But after your remarks there is no longer any need for such labours.

I should just say that the libellum, which you were kind enough to send me, has now encountered its fate. The folder in which it was kept has been purloined from my room in the institute, something that has never happened before and can surely only be explained by the magnetic power exerted by your text and signature. And this same power also makes it extremely unlikely that I shall ever see it again, any more than the prepared lecture text on Kant's practical philosophy[7] which accompanied it. And for all my understanding for the thief, I am rather sad about this.

May I ask how things are going with the second volume of 'Krull'?[8]

From the depths of our hearts we both wish you a speedy recovery, and I wish for myself that I shall soon be seeing you at last.

Greetings to you and yours, from Gretel too,

With heartfelt devotion,

Faithfully yours,
[Teddie Adorno]

SOURCE: O: TS (carbon copy); Theodor W. Adorno Archive, Frankfurt am Main.

1 Thomas Mann had gone to stay in Noordwijk aan Zee in the Netherlands in July 1955. On 23 July he was forced for health reasons to return to Switzerland and stay in the cantonal hospital in Zurich.

2 On 11 July Mann had been received by the Queen of Holland.

3 Adorno is alluding to the figure of Mynheer Peeperkorn, 'an older Dutchman', in chapter VII of Mann's novel *The Magic Mountain*.

4 In the introductory section of his speech on Schiller, Mann had said: 'We wish to pay homage to this beneficent spirit who has risen to Elysian bowers. How shall we do so? Who am I to speak in his praise, confronted as I am by mountains of learned appreciations and analyses which scholarship has reared in the past hundred and fifty years? In my diffidence I am emboldened by only one thing, and that of a rather naive and simple-hearted nature. This is the kinship of experience, the brotherhood, the intimacy which exists among all creative artists, irrespective of stature, epoch or character.' See Thomas Mann, 'Versuch über Schiller', *GW* IX, p. 873; English translation: 'On Schiller', in *Last Essays*, London, 1959, p. 7.

5 Adorno is alluding to the passage where Mann quotes Schiller himself concerning the relationship between his own dramatic works and those of Goethe: ' "But what I have done is to shape my own kind of drama according to my talent. That gives me a certain rank in the genre, simply because it is my own." What an amazing sentence! For is not "art" a general heading, in essence

113

totally abstract, which assumes a new and special being in each of its manifestations? Every incarnation of art is a highly personal special case, and the creator often finds it quite difficult to subsume this special case under the grand general notion of art. Every creative production represents a new and in itself highly artistic adaptation of individual predilections and talents to "art". To be exact, art does not exist; there is only the artist and whatever personal arrangement he may make with his work. In that his work is his own, he necessarily achieves "a certain rank".' See 'Versuch über Schiller', *GW* IX, p. 945; English translation: 'On Schiller', p. 89.

6 The music and drama critic Joachim Kaiser (*b*. 1928) had studied music at Göttingen, Frankfurt am Main and Tübingen. He received his doctorate in Tübingen in 1957 with a dissertation on 'Dramatic Style in Grillparzer'.

7 Adorno had delivered a series of lectures as an 'Introduction to Kant's Critique of Practical Reason' in the winter semester of 1954–5. In the summer of 1955 he also lectured on 'Kant's Transcendental Logic'.

8 Adorno is alluding to the continuation which Mann had been planning for his novel *Confessions of Felix Krull, Confidence Man: Memoirs Part One*, which had appeared in 1954. Mann did not live to complete the work.

42 THOMAS MANN TO THEODOR W. ADORNO
     ZURICH, 30.7.1955

THOMAS MANN   KILCHBERG AM ZÜRICHSEE
                               ALTE LANDSTRASSE 39

                                          Cantonal Hospital
                                                    Zurich
                                             30 July 1955

Dear Dr Adorno,
    Many, many thanks for your letter. Yes, I have been cheated out of a week of lovely weather in Noordwijk, and shall be losing I don't know how many weeks of normal upright life because of this unexpected illness,[1] one wholly alien to me, which I originally thought was rheumatism but which turns out on closer medical examination to be a rather severe circulatory problem, an inflammation in the vein of the left leg. This sort of thing calls for great care, a long period of lying absolutely still (with all the strange and unfamiliar apparatus this involves), and very precise treatment. And I am certainly receiving this perfectly here, under the charge of the well-known specialist in internal medicine Professor Löffler.[2] I do not actually have any pain to speak of, although there are all the minor irritations that tend to accompany a major illness. But these things are so *tedious*. I shall probably not get

114

out within four weeks, and only one has passed already. Pazienza! What I have entered into here is Magic Mountain time.

Something of the kind was only to be expected. I was quite astonished when after the wild life I led in May and June[3] the usual reaction of sickness failed to materialize. Then, when I thought I was recuperating on the magnificent beach in Noordwijk, enjoying my role as Commander of Orange-Nassau[4] ('Je maintiendrai!'), nature had devised something entirely new and surprising for me – namely this. The witty, quietly inventive female!

You will find the Hesses[5] in the Waldhaus, but not me. Even if I should be discharged from here while you are still staying up there, 1800 metres would be quite beyond my limits at the moment. I shall look forward to meeting in Kilchberg, then, on your way back. You will enjoy seeing the house, which in its beautiful location and unpretentious comfort makes the perfect final establishment for me.

Yours,
Thomas Mann

SOURCE: O: MS; Theodor W. Adorno Archive, Frankfurt am Main. Fp: *Briefe III*, p. 415. Written on the back of the envelope in Katia Mann's hand: 'Unfortunately left unposted for three days through an oversight!'

1 The autopsy revealed that the cause of death was a rupture of the lower abdominal artery.

2 The internist Wilhelm Löffler (1887–1972) was director of the medical clinic at the cantonal hospital in Zurich from 1937 until 1957.

3 Mann is referring to 'the Schiller and Lübeck trip' (see *Tagebücher 1953–1955*, pp. 342–5) and the celebrations on the occasion of his eightieth birthday earlier in the year.

4 On 1 July 1955 Mann read his lecture on Schiller at the University of Amsterdam, where he was awarded the Order of Orange-Nassau. The inscription of the Commander Cross reads 'Je maintiendrai!'

5 Hermann Hesse (1877–1962) and his wife, Ninon (1895–1966), lived in Montagnola in Tessin and had been friends of the Manns for many years.

HOTEL WALDHAUS . SILS-MARIA [ENGADIN]

13 August 1955

Dear Madam,

I have just heard the unfathomable news[1] by telephone from Frankfurt. I am at a loss for words – it is a crushing blow. I say only this, something which can perhaps only be uttered at such a moment: I loved him very, very much.

We both feel for you, and with you, at this time,

Unreservedly yours, Teddie Adorno

SOURCE: O: MS with printed hotel letterhead; Thomas Mann Archive, Zurich.

1 Thomas Mann had died at ten o'clock at night on 12 August.

Appendix
Adorno's Notes and Sketches
for Doctor Faustus

Adorno's Sketches for the Chamber Music of Adrian Leverkühn

O: TS (carbon copy); Theodor W. Adorno Archive, Frankfurt am Main.

For the Violin Concerto: It is a 'gentler' piece incorporating the three tonalities of B flat major, C major and D major, the last as a kind of double dominant, the first as a double subdominant, with C major precisely intermediate between the two. The work artfully negotiates these tonalities, the composition constantly suggesting one or other, but never decisively establishing any of them. They are overlaid with one another for extensive parts of the work and C major is only properly established at the very end. The opening movement is marked *Andante amoroso* and characterized by a certain sweetness and gentleness that constantly borders on the ironic. The leading chord is c–g–e–b♭–d–f♯–a – Adrian likes to joke that this all sounds very French to his ears. This effusive movement is followed by an extremely boisterous and virtuosic Scherzo which allows full rein to the instrument's technical possibilities. The final movement consists of a series of colourful and vividly contrasting variations on a theme that is derived from the principal subject of the first movement. Before composing his own piece, Leverkühn has carefully studied the violinistic technique of Bériot, Vieuxtemps and Wieniawski and applies it here in a half-respectful and half-caricatural manner. 'The apotheosis of salon music – it should please the audience, but also leave them with a guilty conscience about it.' The piece also incorporates a quotation from 'The Devil's Trill' by Tartini.

On the music for three strings, three winds, and piano: this is a 'roving' piece with extended and fantastical themes, elaborately developed and never strictly repeated. The whole work is stormy and yearning in character, 'romantic' in tone, but executed with the most rigorous modern means and precisely constructed throughout. The

119

*Adorno's sketch of the Arietta theme from Beethoven's Sonata op. 111
(original Ms in the Thomas Mann Archive, Zurich)*

Here the melody is immersed, so to speak, under the weight
of the chords themselves

the motif in its original,
'objective' form:

the 'humane', valedictory variant at
the end

NB after the close of the first half of the theme the additional,
decisive note is C sharp.

Transcription of the Arietta theme and Adorno's annotations

first movement is entitled 'Fantasy', the second is an Adagio which becomes ever more intense as it unfolds, while the Finale begins lightly and playfully, takes on growing contrapuntal complexity and an increasing expression of tragic gravity, and concludes with a sombre epilogue reminiscent of a funeral march. The piano is never used to provide rich harmonic texture, but treated soloistically as in a piano concerto – effectively echoing the style of the Violin Concerto. The piano part, especially in the last movement, is of extraordinary technical difficulty. The problem of successfully combining the different sonorities throughout the piece is negotiated with enormous subtlety. The winds never drown the strings, but alternate with them and always allow them room to make themselves heard: only rarely do the winds and strings combine as tutti. The whole piece arouses the impression that one starts off on firm ground, but is then gradually enticed into ever more remote regions – everything ends up very different from what was originally expected. Adrian says: I wanted to compose not a sonata, but a novel.

This tendency towards 'prose' finds its most extreme expression in Adrian's most esoteric work, his *String Quartet*. If chamber music generally provides a typical opportunity for thematic-motivic elaboration, this is all expressly and provocatively avoided here. There are no motivic relationships, developments or variations at all – not even repetitions; new material emerges continuously, in an apparently quite unconnected way, linked by similarity of tone or colour, but mostly by contrast. There is no trace of any traditional forms here. It is as if this apparently anarchic composition gave Adrian a breathing space before broaching the symphonic Cantata, the most tautly constructed piece he would ever write. He simply abandons himself here to his own ear, to the inner logic of immediate suggestion. The polyphony is intensified to the highest degree. Each voice is entirely independent at every moment. The whole structure is articulated through very clearly contrasted tempi, although the individual parts of the work are played without interruption so that it can properly be described as a 'single-movement' work. The first part is marked *moderato*, and is a kind of conversation between the four instruments. This leads into a *presto* section with a sense of whispering delirium about it, played by all four instruments muted. There follows a slower, though shorter, section in which the viola takes the principal voice throughout, with various interventions by the other instruments, rather like a vocal composition. Finally, in the last section, marked *allegro con fuoco*, the polyphony comes to full and free expression in extended lines. The piece concludes in a combination of runs and trills, like so many tongues of flame coming together from four different quarters, that creates the impression of an entire orchestra. By exploiting the full range and timbral pos-

122

sibilities of each instrument, the piece acquires a sonority which transcends the usual limits of chamber music altogether. And indeed the critics who found the work a particularly hard nut to crack typically reproached it precisely for being a crypto-orchestral composition. But careful study of the score, and in particular proper performance of the work, would clearly demonstrate that it actually draws upon the most subtle accomplishments of the string quartet genre. And Adrian is convinced anyway that the traditional limits of chamber music and orchestral style can no longer be observed today, that they have tended to coalesce ever since the emancipation of musical colour. And this tendency towards the hybrid, already perceptible in Adrian's treatment of vocal and instrumental writing in his setting of 'The Apocalypse', now becomes stronger and stronger. Adrian says: the academic study of philosophy has already taught me that to posit limits is already to transcend them, and I have always followed this insight. He is an 'old master' in the extreme sense.

123

Adorno's Sketch for Adrian Leverkühn's Cantata 'Doktor Fausti Weheklag'

O: TS (carbon copy); Theodor W. Adorno Archive, Frankfurt am Main.

Notes for *The Lament of Doctor Faustus*

Form of a *lamento*. Effectively non-dynamic, devoid of development.

Large-scale orchestral interludes that appropriately reflect the relationship of the work to its subject matter (like the Funeral March in *The Twilight of the Gods*). The gesture of *Ecce homo*.

Faustus's Descent into Hell conceived in terms of large-scale ballet music. A galloping movement, stylized with the highest rhythmic variety. (Winds and continuo only.)

The conclusion of the work purely orchestral, the chorus gradually introducing a symphonic movement, reversing, as it were, the Ode to Joy, just as Adrian saw his task to lie in repudiating the Ninth Symphony as something that indeed 'should never be'.

The *melodic* character of the whole. More contrapuntal than polyphonic: principal voices in relation to secondary voices. The melodic *core*, from which everything is developed, is the passage underlying the words 'I die a Christian, good and bad'. Extended melodic arcs.

The idea of the lament of the creature, beginning from the subject, but spreading out increasingly to embrace the entire cosmos. The form consists in the constantly renewed levels of this lament. The purely symphonic movement as a lament of God himself: thus I never willed it. The whole piece therefore an enormous *set of variations* – here too negatively related to the Ninth Symphony. Each variation, a movement in itself, corresponds to another circle of the expanding lament, and inevitably introduces a further one. 'Like casting a stone into the

124

water', as Adrian says. Each movement in turn is also a sequence of variations and all derive from the theme of 'I die a Christian, good and bad'. As Adrian says, 'For there is nothing new, that is the lament.'

The highest and most elaborate artistic configuration of the work serves a higher purpose. The order within the material has become absolute. Like heaven and the infernal laughter before, *everything* is now thematic, not a single free note. But the artistic labour now therefore penetrates the material itself. The idea of a fugue would be meaningless here because there are no longer any free notes at all. But this merely serves to *liberate the language*. The artistic labour is complete before the composition really begins, and the latter can now unfold entirely uninhibitedly. But this makes it all the easier to abandon oneself to expression. For *The Lament*, while the strictest of Adrian's works, is also a purely expressive one. On the basis of the pre-organized material, he can uninhibitedly give himself over to subjectivity, unhindered by the pre-given construction of the work. The recourse to Monteverdi, as the beginning of the more modern turn in music, is a reconstruction of expression, and all expression is ultimately a kind of lament. The allegorical origin of expression as 'intention'. Melancholy. Recourse to the most essential manifestations of expression, primordial forms of expression.

All the originally expressive moments of music are now *consciously* deployed, like the sigh, . . . [the original manuscript, which has not survived, probably contained a music example at this point]. The creation of suspensions (naturally simply as rhythmic means), metric chromaticism. (Adrian's references to a chaconne by Jacobo Melani, Riemann II, 2, p. 242ff., literally anticipating a passage from *Tristan*.) Echo effects (every variation is an echo, a transformation of earlier material). Echo-like extensions. Pauses before the beginning of phrases. Repetitions like 'Lasciatemi morire'. Stretched out syllables, tension. *No imitation. Falling* intervals, sinking declamation.

The lamenting of nymphs already found in the settings of *Orfeo* by Peri and Caccini.

Faustus and Orpheus. A lament which quotes from the nether world of the shades.

Everything, even individual parts, chorally conceived. Only Faustus as solo voice (baritone).

'Continuo': constituted by two harps, harpsichord, piano, celesta, glockenspiel and percussion, a kind of constantly accompanying system for the harmony.

After the ballet music an overwhelmingly tragic choral section (a capella with the greatest intensity).

The scene with his pupils is a kind of negative counterpart to the Last Supper. Out of fidelity to his pact with the Devil, he does not *wish* to be saved and repudiates his pupils as tempters. He is right here, because positivity merely represents the world that he scorns.

The idea that questioning negativity stands as an allegory of hope.

The style purer than that of *The Apocalypse*. A sombre tone prevails throughout.

The invocations of Satan.

Each great variation (or 'movement') has its own instrumental ensemble.

Symphonic cantata.

Index

Adorno, Gretel (née Karplus) 32, 41;
  edits Benjamin's *A Berlin Childhood*
  63; on post-war Germany 45
Adorno, Theodor Wiesengrund:
  biographical his own sketch 24–5;
  death of mother 78–89; *Doctor
  Faustus* music and 119–26; on
  fascism in Germany 33–6; first
  contact with Mann vi–viii; 'Four
  Songs to Texts by Stefan George' 11;
  health 109; Horkheimer and 21–2,
  24; Institute for Social Research and
  46; Mann on contribution of 107;
  professorship 61, 63; and Schoenberg
  30–1; in *The Story of a Novel* 21
Against Epistemology (Adorno) *see*
  Towards a Metacritique of
  Epistemology
Akzente (journal) 110, 111
Albersheim, Gerhard 6
Anbruch (journal) 24, 26
anthropogenesis 43–4
anti-Semitism: Nazism 33–6
Archiv für Philosophie (journal) 46, 62
Aron, Betty 32
'The Artist and Society' (Mann) 90, 91
The Authoritarian Personality (Adorno
  et al.) 32, 46-7

'Bach Defended against his Devotees'
  (Adorno) 71, 72, 73, 74
Bahle, Julius: *Eingebung und Tat im
  musikalischen Schaffen* 4
Baudelaire, Charles 96, 98
Bauer-Noeggerath, Marga 44

Beckett, Samuel: 'En attendant Godot'
  107, 109
Beer-Hoffman, Richard 59
Beethoven, Ludwig van: Adorno on 5,
  25; in *Doctor Faustus* 13–14, 15;
  Fidelio 10–11; Piano Sonata, op. 31,
  no 2 5; Piano Sonata, op. 111 5
  120, 121
Beethoven: The Philosophy of Music
  (Adorno) 25, 27
Benjamin, Walter: Adorno and
  Horkheimer's tribute to 24, 26;
  Adorno's portrait of 54–5, 56, 57; *A
  Berlin Childhood* 61, 63
Berg, Alban vii, 4, 24, 26, 30
Bergson, Henri 10
A Berlin Childhood (Benjamin) 61,
  63
Bermann-Fischer, Gottfried 46, 48, 53,
  72–3, 106; Adorno's Kafka lecture
  57
The Betrayed One (Mann) viii, 101-5,
  106-7, 110, 111
Beverly Wilshire Hotel 41
The Black Swan *see* The Betrayed One
The Blue Angel/Professor Unrat (H.
  Mann) 74–7
Blunck, Richard 107
Boyer, Jean 86
Brandes, Georg 58, 59–60
Brod, Max 53, 55, 59
Brück, Max von 60
Brüning, Heinrich 78, 79, 81
Buddenbrooks (Mann) 10-11, 12, 13
Busoni, Ferruccio 8

127